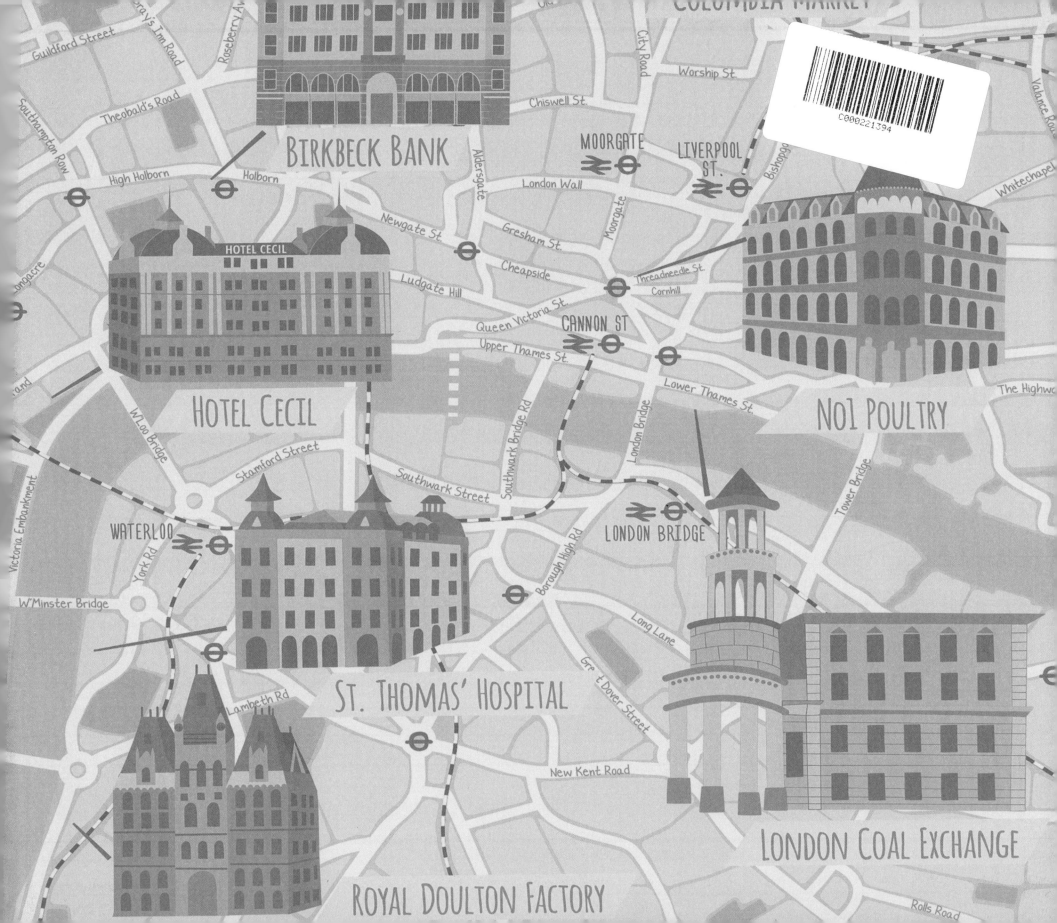

LONDONIST
MAPPED

Published by AA Publishing, a trading name of AA Media Limited,
Fanum House, Basing View, Basingstoke, Hampshire RG21 4EA, UK

First published in 2017
10 9 8 7 6 5 4 3 2

© AA Media Ltd 2017

All text originally published on londonist.com © Londonist Ltd
Additional text © AA Media Ltd

For a full list of illustrators, contributors and copyright holders see page 96

A CIP catalogue record for this book is available from the British Library

ISBN: 978-0-7495-7910-4

Editor: Rebecca Needes
Designer: Elizabeth Baldin
Concept design: Ben Brannan
Repro: Ian Little
Production: Jade Pickard
Art director: James Tims

Printed and bound in Dubai by Oriental Press

This book was typeset in Garden Essential and Plantain Light

A05616

Visit AA Publishing at shop.theAA.com

CONTENTS

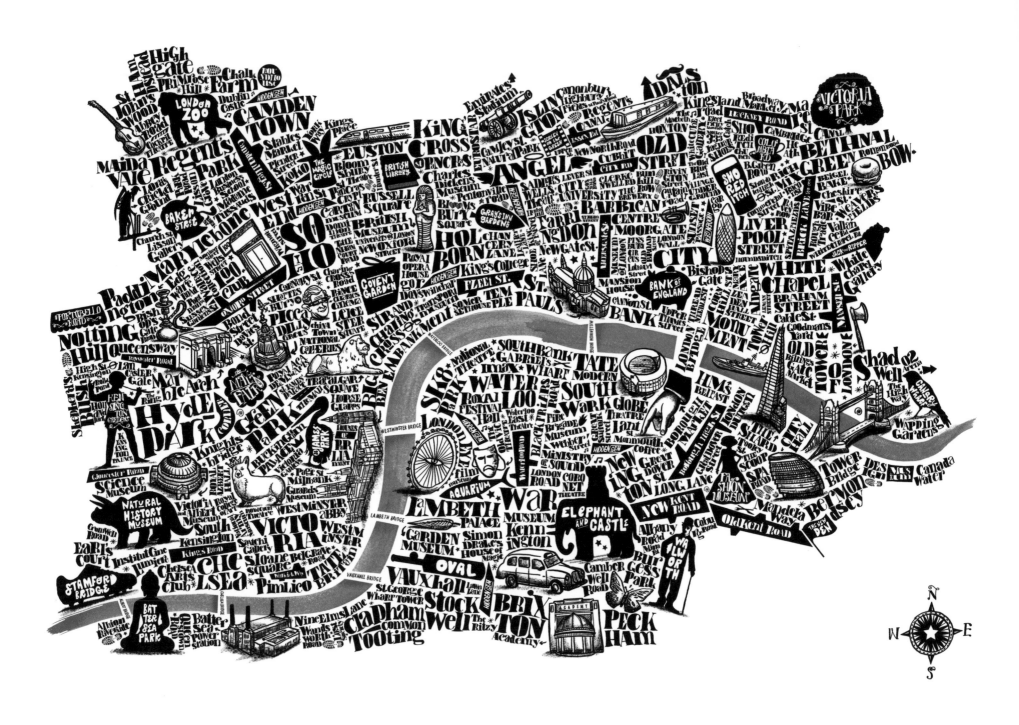

Map by
João Lauro Fonte

FOREWORD

It's Monday morning in the Londonist office. Someone sips their first coffee of the week. Then they frown. Scratch their head. Open their mouth. Look around the room. Close their mouth. Pause, as if concerned they might be about to say something stupid. Then they say it anyway: 'How deep does London go?' they ask no one in particular.

Thus an idea for an article is born. Yes, some of these conversations take place over a pint of beer, rather than a cup of coffee. And yes, some of the questions will be stupid (especially those involving too much beer). But the essence is always the same; there's always something about London we want to know – always something that we must get to the bottom of.

This book is inspired by some of the very best of those questions, and the subsequent articles we wrote.

If you're after a chronology or themes in this book, don't look too hard. While the first and last topics rather neatly bookend the whole thing (so to speak), the rest is a dizzying journey that warps and wefts, ducks and dives all over the place. After all, when he was attempting to rebuild the city following the Great Fire, Christopher Wren famously discovered that you can't curate London to your own liking… it's happy curating itself, thank you.

Yes, we're comparing ourselves to Christopher Wren now.

Anyway, it's for this reason that in this book you'll find a section on dinosaur hunting next to one about the bits of old London Bridge that are scattered over the city. And a section about the 'Magnificent Seven' cemeteries next to a piece on tube pedantry. We meet a lot of pedants in our line of work.

It's not all about trivia, though. Often, in this hard-boiled city of ours, you feel the need to rest on your oars. So we'll also reveal where to find secret gardens, how to booze like a banker – and how to eat, drink and smoke like Winston Churchill. (We cannot be held responsible for the loss of your job.)

We've even dedicated two pages to really terrible jokes about London, which you may or may not thank us for.

Helping us bring the verve and vigor of London to life are a coterie of top-notch illustrators, who have frankly blown our minds with their accompanying images. You could bury your peepers in these illustrations for months, and you still won't have picked out all the intricate and ingenious details.

Speaking of which – you may come across the occasional spelling mistake in the illustrations. On our travels, *Londonist* have delighted in happening upon signs for 'Charring Cross'; a place called 'The School of Englis'; and a misspelling for a vegetable samosa that we cannot repeat here. We love typos so much, we decided to keep ours in… see, now you're going to be studying these illustrations *really* closely.

As for any pedants reading: for once, *Londonist* is in print – not online. That means we don't have a comments section at the bottom of the page. But feel free to get out a pen and scribble your thoughts/questions/grievances on your copy anyway.

We'll get back to you when we can.

Who are *Londonist*?

Established as *The Big Smoker* in 2004, *Londonist* has become one of the go-to places for Londoners and people visiting London. Events, food and drink, history, transport, trivia – we cover everything you need to know about the capital, celebrating its quirks, eccentricities, hidden and surprising bits along the way.

Check us out:

londonist.com

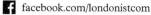 facebook.com/londonistcom

 @londonist

 londonist_com

ABOUT THE MAP

This is the bit where we tell you about the map we've chosen to display alongside each topic, and how it may – or may not – connect with the subject matter. To get you started, here's João Lauro Fonte's typographic map of London. We like how he's picked different locations out to highlight, and the sense of character he gives them – check out the 'hidden gem' flags also. We think it's a great way to kick things off, and a little gem all of its own.

HOW LONDON BECAME LONDON

London has not always been London. Successive occupants have used their own phrases for the city. Some are mythical, some are historical and some are vaguely insulting.

Ancient names

People lived in the area we now call London long before the Romans arrived. For millennia, small tribes would have ranged across the land and fished in the Thames. Several prehistoric structures have been discovered. It's possible to see 6,000-year-old timbers during very low tide at Vauxhall, for example. Yet no strong evidence of permanent settlement has ever been found.

With no settled population, perhaps the region had no name until the Romans founded the city around 43AD. However, it's unlikely that the Romans conjured their name of Londinium from nowhere. Some linguists suggest that they adapted an existing name, possibly Plowonida, from the pre-Celtic words *plew* and *nejd*, which together suggest a wide, flowing river (i.e. the Thames). This then became Lowonidonjon in Celtic times, and eventually Londinium. Another theory suggests a Celtic place name of Londinion, either derived from the name of a local chieftain, or the Celtic word *lond* (meaning 'wild'). There is no consensus and, in the absence of written records, we will probably never know.

Mythical founding

12th-century scholar Geoffrey of Monmouth is responsible for one of London's best known origin myths. He tells us that the city was founded by Brutus, an exiled Trojan, who named his new stronghold Troia Nova (New Troy). Over time, according to Geoffrey, this became Trinovantum. There's a whiff of non-fiction about this. The Trinovantes were one of the pre-eminent local tribes encountered by the Romans. Our medieval cleric was probably indulging in some creative wordplay, back-forming Trinovantes into Troia Nova and thence making up the whole Troy origin thing (or else repeating lost sources who did this).

Roman London

We now step back into verified historical territory. The Romans founded the first known settlement of any note in 43AD, and at some point soon after called it Londinium. The first written record comes from around 117AD, when Tacitus tells us 'Londinium… though undistinguished by the name of a colonia, was much frequented by a number of merchants and trading vessels.' Other sources referring to the city by its Roman name are surprisingly rare, but include grammatical and syntactical variations such as Londinio, Londiniensi and Londiniensium. Around the year 368, the city was renamed Augusta, seen on numerous coins from the era.

Anglo-Saxon London

Roman domination of London effectively ended in 410, when the legions were withdrawn to tackle some pressing domestic matters (Rome was being sacked). We know very little about London over the next two hundred years. The city inside the Roman walls was at some point abandoned. Germanic tribes, whom we now call Anglo-Saxons, took over the area and established a colony around Aldwych and Covent Garden. Sources from the 7th and 8th centuries name this port as Lundenwic, which means 'London settlement or trading town'. In the year 886, Alfred the Great resettled the land inside the still-standing Roman walls, and shored up the defences. The rejuvenated stronghold was known as Lundenburh, meaning the fortified town of London.

London arises

The city slowly grew around Alfred's City and the religious centre of Westminster. Following the Norman Conquest, records begin to show the area referred to by its modern name, or similar versions such as Lundin, Londoun, Lunden and Londen. Over the centuries, the spelling settled down on London. However, the geographic definition of 'London' has changed over the years. Until recent centuries, places such as Westminster or Southwark would have been considered distinct from 'London', the name for the Square Mile within the old Roman walls. Even today, we refer to this area as The City of London, a city within a city.

Nicknames for London

As well as official names, the capital has also attracted a number of sobriquets over the years. Probably the most famous is The Big Smoke, The Old Smoke, or simply The Smoke. These names refer to the dense fogs and smogs that would permeate the city from ancient times. These were greatly exacerbated by the Industrial Revolution and the incredible growth of 19th-century London, which created millions of new chimneys. The name was revived in the 1950s, when the city's worst ever smogs claimed thousands of lives.

Another, less well known nickname for London is The Great Wen. A 'wen' is what today we'd call a sebaceous cyst. The phrase was coined in the 1820s by William Cobbett, who was comparing the rapidly growing city to a biological swelling.

Perhaps in an age dominated by rapid communications and time-poor typing, London will eventually be officially contracted to LDN, a name gaining traction in recent years on the back of other city abbreviations like NYC and LA.

ABOUT THE MAP

This is a map of pure ambition and dedication: Jenni Sparks collaborated with Evermade.com with the aim to create the definitive culture map of London – it took more than two months of intensive research before even starting the illustration process. It's beautifully detailed, as you can see from the small section reproduced here.

Map by
JENNI SPARKS | FULL MAP AT EVERMADE.COM

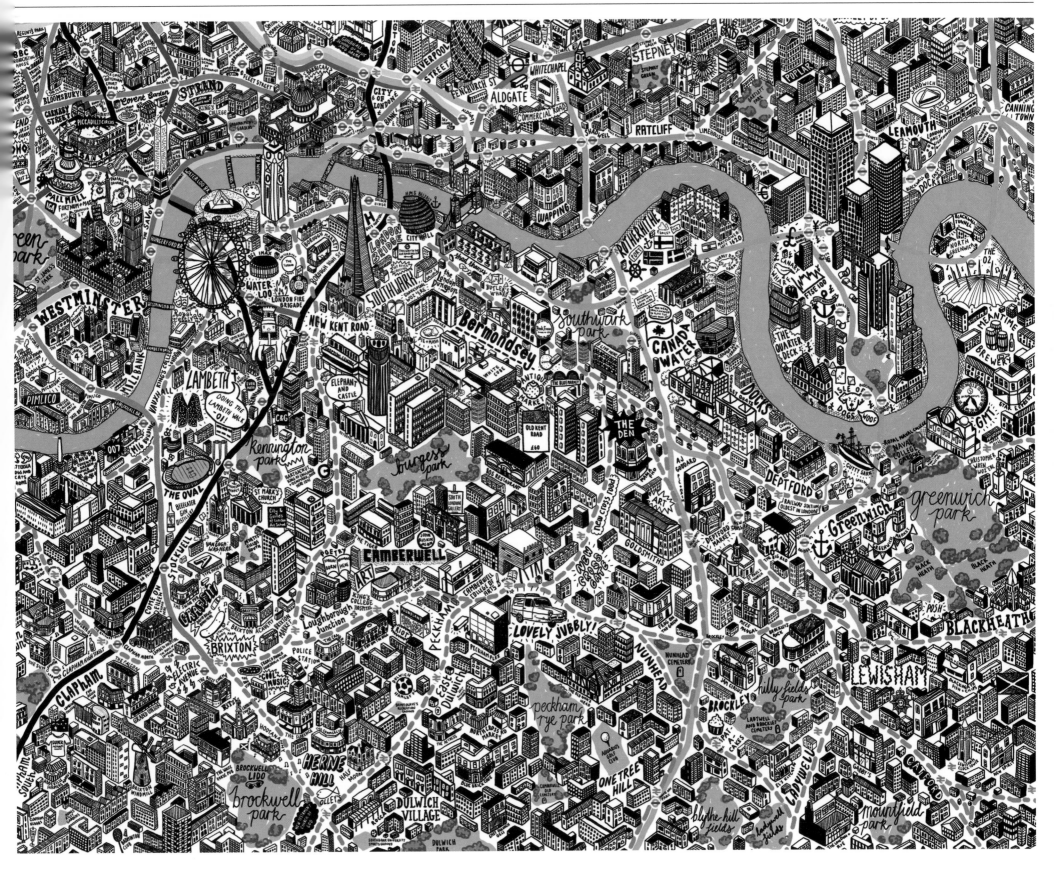

SECRETS OF BUCKINGHAM PALACE

Buckingham Palace is a pretty big place, consisting of 775 rooms (including 19 State rooms, 52 Royal and guest bedrooms, 188 staff bedrooms, 92 offices and 78 bathrooms) and the largest private garden in London, covering 39 acres. The staff – more than 800 of them – can make use of the Court Post Office within the palace, run by Royal Mail. The palace even has its own ATM, and rumour has it that there's a swimming pool, doctor's office and cinema in there too. We look at some little-known facts about the royal residence.

Map by
REBECCA HOWARD ILLUSTRATION

Oldest part

The oldest part of the palace is the wine vaults located below the west wing, dating back to 1760. Back then, it belonged to the family of the Duke of Buckingham and was known as Buckingham House. In 1761, George III acquired the building for the royal family, although it didn't become an official royal residence until years later. Buckingham House was once considered as a potential site for the British Museum, but rejected as too expensive.

Marble Arch

Marble Arch now sits at the northeast corner of Hyde Park, but it was originally built in front of Buckingham Palace. Queen Victoria was the first sovereign to use the palace as her official residence, and it soon became clear that it wasn't large enough for hosting official visitors. So, Marble Arch was moved in order for the fourth wing of the Palace to be built where it once stood.

Down by the river

The 'lost' River Tyburn runs right below the palace, although it's now more of a sewer than a river. In theory it passes underneath the south wing and front courtyard, but we don't fancy going down there to confirm it.

The tunnel rumours

Rumours of tunnels linking Buckingham Palace to various other parts of London are prevalent, though we think it's unlikely that a tunnel exists linking the palace to the tube. An underground link-up with Whitehall and the Houses of Parliament is plausible, given the warren of Whitehall tunnels that is known to exist, but unproven.

Other unproven rumours include a tunnel between the palace and Clarence House, and a branch of the Post Office Railway running right under the palace.

Royal births and deaths

Only one monarch was both born in the palace and died there: Edward VII. More recently, Queen Elizabeth II, gave birth to the Prince of Wales and Prince Andrew at the palace.

A royal assassination attempt

Constitution Hill separates Buckingham Palace from Green Park. It got its name as it was where King Charles II used to take his afternoon walks, or constitutional.

In June 1840, an assassination attempt was made on Queen Victoria as she and Prince Albert rode in a carriage along Constitution Hill. The would-be assassin, Edward Oxford, leant against a fence waiting for the royal couple before drawing a pistol and firing off shots when they arrived. Luckily he missed, and the royal couple were whisked off before any harm could come to them. Oxford was acquitted of treason on the grounds of insanity and sent to the State Criminal Lunatic Asylum in Bethlem.

The balcony

The famous balcony has hosted various members of the royal clan on all manner of occasions. The tradition of the Royals appearing on the balcony began with Queen Victoria, who made an appearance there for the opening of the Great Exhibition in Hyde Park in 1851. The appearance at the end of the Trooping the Colour celebrations was a tradition introduced by George IV.

Behind the scenes

When a state banquet is held at the palace, it can take up to five days to put together the banqueting table and lay it up ready for the occasion. The Queen personally inspects the setup herself.

During the war

Buckingham Palace wasn't immune to the effects of the Blitz. It was hit nine times, some of them when King George VI and Queen Elizabeth (later the Queen Mother) were in residence. The Palace Chapel was destroyed by a direct hit in 1940, at which Queen Elizabeth was reported to have said 'I'm glad we've been bombed. It makes me feel I can look the East End in the face.'

Speaking of wars, today the lake outside is one of St James's Park's most prominent features, but for six years last century, it didn't exist. The lake was drained in 1916 to allow temporary government buildings to be built there in World War I. Ministry of Shipping buildings remained there until the lake was filled with water again in 1922.

London's oldest helicopter pad

The garden is the oldest helicopter pad in London – sort of. A helicopter was first landed in the garden just before the Queen's Coronation in 1953, not on an official helipad, but in a helicopter landing area, which continued to be used for many years.

ABOUT THE MAP

It's impossible to look at this map without seeing Buckingham Palace dominate. There's plenty more to see, though – including some tiny Piccadilly Circus lights, and some mounted Queen's Guards at Whitehall. We're fans.

LONDON'S BEST UNSUNG MUSEUMS

London has a wealth of museums, covering just about every subject imaginable; if you can name it, there's probably a display case or two dedicated to it somewhere. The likes of the Natural History Museum, the Science Museum and the British Museum are well-trodden tourist trails, but what about some of the lesser-known gems? Overleaf is our pick of some of London's best unsung museums.

Map by
CAROLINE HARPER

ABOUT THE MAP

We have no idea how Caroline Harper managed to pack so many museums into one map, but it's quite the tour de force. If anyone ever manages to visit the whole lot, let us know.

London — A MISCELLANY of MUSEUMS

BATTLE OF BRITAIN Museum Harrow

museum of DOMESTIC DESIGN & ARCHITECTURE

ROYAL AIR FORCE MUSEUM Hendon

OLD SPEECH ROOM GALLERY Harrow

CAMDEN ARTS CENTRE

← Southall Railway Centre

LONDON MOTOR MUSEUM Hillingdon

LONDON motorcycle museum

LOUISE T BLOUIN foundation

MUSEUM of BRANDS, PACKAGING & ADVERTISING

ALEXANDER FLEMING LAB MUSEUM

PITZHANGER

LEIGHTON HOUSE MUSEUM

STAFFORD TERRACE

KENSINGTON PALACE

SERPENTINE

V&A

BOSTON MANOR HOUSE

GUNNERSBURY PK MUSEUM

KEW BRIDGE STEAM museum

Hogarth's House BEER STREET

BADEN POWELL COLLECTION

RCM MUSEUM of MUSIC

HAMMERSMITH TERRACE

OSTERLEY PARK & HOUSE

KELMSCOTT HOUSE

DIPPY NATURAL HISTORY

CARLYLE'S HOUSE

CHELSEA PHYSIC Garden founded 1673

Musical Museum

KEW PALACE

Syon House

Fulham Palace

Fear Naught

CHISWICK HOUSE

RUGBY MUSEUM

Marianne North Gallery

Queen Charlotte Cottage

MUSEUM of RICHMOND

THE DE MORGAN FOUNDATION

GARRICK'S TEMPLE

THE ROYAL MILITARY SCHOOL of MUSIC

White Lodge & Ballet Resource

WANDSWORTH MUSEUM

Orleans House

Marble Hill

WIMBLEDON WINDMILL MUSEUM

WIMBLEDON LAWN TENNIS MUSEUM

KINGSTON MUSEUM

HAM HOUSE

PORCH HOUSE

SOUTHSIDE HS

NONSUCH MANOR

North

Venture beyond the Wellcome Collection and the Jewish Museum in north London and you'll find a number of great museums – most of them in storied locations – celebrating the cultures that grew out of industry on London's waterways, the city's Jewish heritage and the World War II secrets you won't find in the bunkers of Westminster.

Markfield Beam Engine and Museum

The gorgeous steam engine at the Markfield Museum is decorated with Doric columns and acanthus leaves with flywheels 27 feet tall – its majesty belying the fact it used to pump sewage around town.

Now defunct, the engine still stands in its engine house in a quiet park just off the A10. It's open on the second Sunday of the month (plus the fourth Sunday in the summer) and sometimes they even turn on the steam so you can see it work. If you're interested in Victoriana, it's a bit of a hidden treasure.

2 Willow Road

This Hampstead property is often overlooked for the impressive Fenton House and Hampstead pergolas nearby. But anyone with an interest in 20th-century art and architecture should indulge their nosy side by wandering around Trellick Tower architect Erno Goldfinger's former home, and the only modernist house in London that's open to the public.

It's filled with furniture Goldfinger designed himself, alongside art by Bridget Riley, Marcel Duchamp, Henry Moore and Max Ernst. Instead of wandering around the flat, visitors get guided tours – a great chance to learn and ask questions in a way museum visitors don't often get the chance to.

Keats House

Literary London is so often thought of as Dickens's dank, dark city of inequality and hardship. But what about the London of a medical student-turned-poet? See the engagement ring and love letters Keats gave to his fiancée, and his death mask, as well as manuscripts of his work and books from his library.

This museum offers visitors a great way to find out about early 18th-century London, life in the middle-classes back then, and the landmarks in Hampstead where Keats went to write.

Bruce Castle

From the civilian internees at Alexandra Palace to Tottenham's Speedway engine factory to its Roman settlement, there's more at Bruce Castle Museum than you'd expect.

The building itself (along with its lovely grounds) has its own strange story: it was a private home from the 16th century, then a school and a doctor's surgery. Perhaps a bit niche for many Londoners, but there are plenty of good resources here for anyone with an interest in local history.

Canal Museum

If you've ever enjoyed a walk or bike ride along one of the city's waterways, this museum explains why they've got such a pride of place in contemporary London.

It's also, surprisingly, a great place for anyone who has a passion for ice cream: the museum sits in the warehouse of a late 19th-century ice cream baron called Carlo Gatti who imported Norwegian ice for his food business, and still has an ice well in the basement that particle physicists use for experiments.

Freud Museum

For anyone who's ever wondered whether a cigar is just a cigar… The Freud Museum has recreated the therapist's office, including the couch and Freud's collected figurines of characters from myths and classical religion.

The museum regularly runs great arts and cultural classes, courses and talks that are brilliant for writers and artists with an interest in the creative role of the unconscious. For everyone else, this museum is a great place to look at how the roles of analysis and mental health care have diverged – and to make as many innuendoes as your visit allows.

The RAF Museum

Sit in the cockpit of a Spitfire at the RAF Museum and find out how British planes helped win the World Wars. This enormous site has hangars and halls of aircraft to see, as well as detailed exhibits about pilots and pioneers, speeches and films.

Ben Uri Gallery, also known as The Art Museum For Everyone

London's Jewish museum is unmissable, and if you want to find out more about Jewish heritage in London then this Kilburn spot is a great next trip. More than 100 years old, the gallery has a collection of around 1,000 20th-century paintings and photographs including work by Frank Auerbach and the Whitechapel Boys.

South

We all love the walrus and other beasts stuffed into the Horniman Museum and the nautical delights of Greenwich's Maritime Museum, but south London has plenty of other museums hanging around the edges of parks and loitering down side streets.

Bethlem Museum of the Mind

Opened by Grayson Perry in March 2015, the Bethlem Museum of the Mind is placed within the current location for the Bethlem Royal Hospital, historically known as Bedlam. Visitors are greeted by statues that once lay above the old doors of the hospital, depicting the Victorian idea of madness. One gazes inanely, the other is chained and tormented.

Straitjackets and medicine bottles are on display but the overall emphasis of the museum is on the lives and creativity of people within the mental health system and the places, good or bad, that they occupy in the wider world. Everything here is presented with sensitivity and respect for the troubled souls who have passed through Bedlam and other institutions.

The Cinema Museum

A feature off a street, then off another street near the Elephant and Castle is the Cinema Museum. It's mostly a museum of cinemas themselves, their history and architecture, lighting, seating and carpets as well as the uniforms their staff wore (with so many shiny buttons).

There's also cinematic ephemera: the collection began with co-founder Ronald Grant's lobby card collection, including posters, classic style 3D glasses and other pieces of film history. Alongside the cinema history, these carry with them a history of branding and design.

The museum also has its own cinema which hosts regular screenings and events.

Wimbledon Windmill Museum

The Wimbledon Windmill Museum nestles among the bushes and shrubs of Wimbledon Common. You can immerse yourself in the diorama depicting the construction of the windmill around 1817 and the general exhibition of windmills, milling and bread making. The windmill also has a cabinet dedicated to Scouts founder Robert Baden-Powell's seminal *Scouting for Boys*, which was partly written within the windmill.

The Museum of Croydon

No sniggering you. Croydon has a long and fascinating human history – look, stop it – which is depicted in the Clock Tower museum.

There's plenty of cultural ephemera to spot, including books by Croydon-born sex researcher Henry Havelock Ellis, an unexploded bomb shell from World War II, some Bridget Riley op-art, a 'Trojan' bubble car and exhibits dedicated to extraordinary people who have lived, loved and made a difference in Croydon: drills, glasses, books. It's a fine example of what a local museum could and should be.

West

The South Kensington museums are rightly regarded among the best in the world, yet are often too busy to appreciate properly. Delve a little deeper into west London, however, and you'll find a couple of dozen smaller museums, many of which get very little publicity.

Boston Manor House

West London has no shortage of big houses to explore, from Chiswick to Syon to Osterley. Smaller, but perhaps more characterful is Boston Manor House, a Jacobean mansion on the banks of the River Brent. Start by exploring the grounds; the ancient cedars and yews are truly remarkable. Inside, a range of panelled rooms culminates in the upstairs State Rooms, where we swear the angels are modelled on Margaret Thatcher.

Hogarth's House

The great satirist and painter considered this Chiswick pile his country retreat. It now lurks beside the roaring Hogarth Roundabout. The house museum, restored in 2011, offers plenty of insights into Hogarth's family life and career. Look out, too, for the characterful statue of the painter and his dog, on Chiswick High Road, and his final resting place in St Nicholas's churchyard.

London Motor Museum

If you thought London only had one transport museum, think again. As well as the magnificent Whitewebbs to the north of the capital, fans of throbbing engines might also pay a visit to this Hayes attraction. Exhibits include a pair of Batmobiles, a 'paddock' of supercars and more than 200 other vehicles, as well as a restaurant in a bus.

London Museum of Water & Steam

This former water-pumping station contains a set of humongous Victorian engines that still 'steam up' every weekend, and a landmark tower that makes this the most visible small museum in London. The wider museum tells the story of London's water provision, with plenty of antiquated kit to behold. A 2014 refresh has turned this into one of the best local museums around, even if its name is somewhat tautological. You'll spot it marked on the map as Kew Bridge Steam Museum.

Museum of Brands, Packaging and Advertising

This seemingly recherché museum, opened around 15 years ago, has been such a success that it had to move address to cope with visitor numbers. It is probably the most famous museum in this line-up. The collection of packaging plays heavily on our collective nostalgia, with visitors of all generations declaring 'oh look, I remember that' at an antique gravy tin or long-forgotten sweet wrapper.

Musical Museum

Next to the London Museum of Water & Steam, the Musical Museum celebrates engineering of a different persuasion. The scope of the museum is narrower than the name implies; its collection focuses on self-playing instruments, 'from the tiniest of clockwork music boxes to the Mighty Wurlitzer'. Look out for film screenings and free concerts.

East

Once you've exhausted the Geffrye Museum and the V&A's Museum of Childhood, there are still dozens of museums in east London to try, many of them unsung. The area's history as a magnet for migrants and industry, its working class heritage and the legacy of its activists all co-exist alongside medical museums, artists' houses, and Tudor and Georgian houses that the Luftwaffe missed.

Museum of London Docklands

Canary Wharf was not much of a weekend destination, for obvious reasons, until this Museum of London outpost opened. The main story it tells is that of the workers, slaves and servants who were vital to keeping the British Empire ticking over.

Sutton House, Hackney

See the clash of cultures as squatter graffiti marks Hackney history on the walls of this Tudor house. Sutton House was owned by Ralph Sadler (yep, of *Wolf Hall* fame) and changed hands several times before the National Trust got hold of it. The curators here run a brilliant events programme – keep an eye on the website for details.

Museum of Immigration, Spitalfields

A clandestine synagogue is just part of the story of this little Princelet Street museum, which documents the secret life and previously untold stories of London's immigrant communities, including Huguenots, Jews and Bangladeshi migrants. East London owes so much of its heritage to the people who migrated, and the communities who went before them.

Dennis Severs' House

Installed not as a museum but a still-life drama, this house museum feels uncanny, as if its occupants had just popped out for a moment. Each room tells a different story of a family of (French) Huguenot weavers who moved to London in 1724. Many visitors have highlighted the candlelit evening tours in winter as particularly atmospheric.

Ragged School Museum

If you think school sucks now, you should have seen it in Victorian times. Some dedicated souls have restored this Bow institution so that visitors can experience chalkboards and learning by rote firsthand. Thomas Barnardo stopped off in London to train as a doctor and missionary, but after seeing the state of the East End he set up a school here in 1867. Locals saved the building from demolition in the 1980s – find out why they were so passionate about the legacy on a visit.

Vestry House

Walthamstow residents know and love the William Morris Gallery (below), but this gem is often overlooked. First a workhouse, then a police station, it became a museum back in 1931. It's great for residents who want to find out more about local history, but it is also good for exhibitions by contemporary local photographers. Don't miss the garden when you visit.

Royal London Hospital Museum

So you've been to the Wellcome Collection, Old Operating Theatre, Barts Museum of Pathology and the Hunterian? Time to head to this Whitechapel crypt. A replica of Joseph Merrick, *aka* the Elephant Man's skeleton leans forlornly in one of the cabinets, plus you can read all about the stories of hero nurses Edith Cavell and Eva Luckes, and check out surgical equipment of yore.

William Morris Gallery

Although this gallery's on the radar for many east Londoners, it couldn't be left off the list. Morris's former home now hosts permanent galleries of his work (check out the sketch of him on a fat little Icelandic pony, upstairs), as well as temporary exhibitions.

WHY DOES LONDON HAVE SO MANY ROYAL PARKS?

It's often said that London is one of the greenest cities in Europe, possibly the world – and London's eight Royal Parks go some way to upping the city's green credentials. They cover a total of 5,000 acres – but how did so much of London end up as a Royal Park?

Map by
KATHERINE BAXTER FOR LONDONTOWN.COM

Greenwich Park

One of the only Royal Parks to predate Henry VIII's turbulent reign, Greenwich Park was inherited by Henry V's brother in 1427 and was passed down through generations of monarchs. Each added their own touch: Henry VIII introduced deer to the park (a small deer enclosure remains today – though you can no longer shoot them with arrows), James I's wife Queen Anne had the Queen's House built, and Charles II commissioned Christopher Wren to build the Royal Observatory.

St James's Park

St James's Park seems the most obvious choice for a Royal Park, given that it's overlooked by the front windows of Buckingham Palace. But it predates the palace by many centuries.

It takes its name from a leper hospital which was built on the site in the 13th century, but the land was claimed by Henry VIII in 1532, and used to fulfil his hunting needs (he had serious hunting needs). The park itself wasn't considered big enough to be used as a hunting ground, so he put it to use as an area for breeding young deer – once they were old enough, they were shipped off to Hyde Park and Regent's Park to face their fate.

Green Park

The history of Green Park is a little hazier than some of the other Royal Parks. The first record of its existence dates back to 1554, although it was known as Upper St James's Park until around 1746, suggesting it was part of the original St James's Park seized by Henry VIII in 1532.

Regent's Park

Regent's Park was previously known as Marylebone Park – and, prior to that, it belonged to Barking Abbey. Henry VIII seized the land in the late 1530s and used it as a hunting ground. It was redeveloped by John Nash in the 1800s at the same time as nearby Regent Street.

Hyde Park

The largest Royal Park, Hyde Park was also seized by Henry VIII in 1536 as part of his Dissolution of the Monasteries. Not content with one central London hunting ground – and a deer breeding ground – he took to the saddle in Hyde Park too. It remained private until King James I allowed limited public access and, in 1637, King Charles I allowed complete public access.

Kensington Gardens

Kensington Gardens was originally part of the neighbouring Hyde Park, and was part of the land that Henry VIII put to use as a hunting ground. The two parks weren't separated until 1728, when Queen Caroline wanted to create a more formal landscape garden.

Bushy Park

Henry VIII acquired this land from Cardinal Wolsey at the same time as nearby Hampton Court Palace. At the time the area now known as Bushy Park was composed of three smaller parks: Hare Warren, Middle Park and Bushy Park. Once again, the King put the land to use as a hunting ground.

Richmond Park

Richmond Park is known for its deer herds today so it'll come as no surprise that it was established as a deer park, although this time – gasp – Henry VIII wasn't involved. Charles I brought his court to Richmond Palace in 1625 to escape the plague, and established the deer park nearby. His decision to enclose the land in 1637 wasn't popular with locals, so as a compromise he allowed pedestrian access.

When Charles I was executed in 1649, the park was passed to the City of London Corporation, but was returned to royalty when Charles II returned to London in 1660.

Hampton Court Park (Home Park)

The sharp-eyed among you will have realised we're now onto our ninth of the eight Royal Parks. Hampton Court Park (also known as Home Park) is a special case in that it is a Royal Park, but it's managed by Historic Royal Palaces as part of Hampton Court Palace, and not by the Royal Parks organisations.

How it came to be a Royal Park is pretty straightforward – the palace was built for Cardinal Thomas Wolsey in 1515, but when he and Henry VIII fell out over Wolsey's failure to get the king's marriage to Catherine of Aragon annulled in 1529, Henry seized the palace for himself, including the surrounding parkland (which, unsurprisingly given his track record, he converted into hunting grounds). The formal gardens surrounding the palace are covered by the palace admission charge, but the rest of Hampton Court Park is separate and is free to visit.

ABOUT THE MAP

According to Greenspace Information for Greater London, London has over 3,000 parks, and roughly 47% of London is considered to be green space (this includes private gardens, as well as public spaces such as parks, sports facilities and cemeteries). Katherine Baxter has managed to pack around 70 of them (we admit, we lost count) into her London Parks map, which we think is pretty impressive.

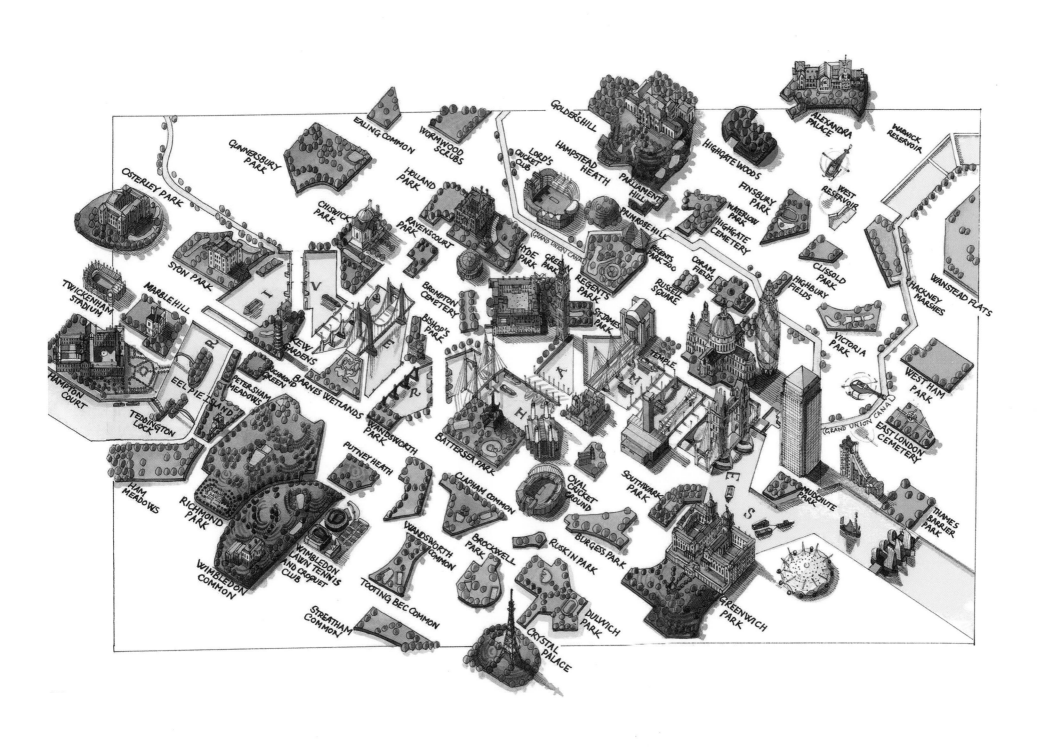

OSTERLEY PARK

GUNNERSBURY PARK

EALING COMMON

WORMWOOD SCRUBS

GOLDERS HILL

ALEXANDRA PALACE

WARWICK RESERVOIR

HAMPSTEAD HEATH

HIGHGATE WOODS

PARLIAMENT HILL

FINSBURY PARK

WEST RESERVOIR

HOLLAND PARK

LORD'S CRICKET CLUB

PRIMROSE HILL

WATERLOW PARK

HIGHGATE CEMETERY

CHISWICK PARK

RAVENSCOURT PARK

HYDE PARK

GREEN PARK

REGENT'S PARK

REGENT'S PARK ZOO

CORAM FIELDS

CLISSOLD PARK

HIGHBURY FIELDS

WANSTEAD FLATS

SYON PARK

BROMPTON CEMETERY

ST JAMES PARK

RUSSELL SQUARE

HACKNEY MARSHES

TWICKENHAM STADIUM

MARBLE HILL

KEW GARDENS

BISHOP'S PARK

TEMPLE

VICTORIA PARK

WEST HAM PARK

HAMPTON COURT

EEL PIE ISLAND

PETERSHAM MEADOWS

RICHMOND GREEN

BARNES WETLANDS

WANDSWORTH PARK

BATTERSEA PARK

GRAND UNION CANAL

EAST LONDON CEMETERY

TEDDINGTON LOCK

HAM MEADOWS

RICHMOND PARK

PUTNEY HEATH

OVAL CRICKET GROUND

SOUTHWARK PARK

MUDCHUTE PARK

THAMES BARRIER PARK

WIMBLEDON LAWN TENNIS AND CROQUET CLUB

CLAPHAM COMMON

BURGESS PARK

WIMBLEDON COMMON

WANDSWORTH COMMON

BROCKWELL PARK

RUSKIN PARK

GREENWICH PARK

TOOTING BEC COMMON

DULWICH PARK

STREATHAM COMMON

CRYSTAL PALACE

A BRIEF GUIDE TO LONDON'S DOCKS

Historically, London's status as a port was key to its prosperity. Ships traditionally docked at the many riverside wharves located on the Pool of London – that part of the Thames immediately downriver from London Bridge. Although this had served as London's main port since Roman times, the Pool gave little protection from the elements and suffered from a lack of quayside space. To get around this, purpose-built docks were constructed along the Thames to unload cargoes – a process which reached its zenith in the 19th century.

Map by
LUKE AGBAIMONI

The docks were badly damaged during World War II and their use declined thereafter due to the rise of container shipping (which needed bigger docks and didn't require the labour-intensive unloading and storage processes which characterised London's docks). Most of them closed between 1967 and 1981, but the names of some of them live on in the new developments (including some DLR stations) that have sprung up where they once stood.

Queenhithe Dock

This ancient quay, upstream from London Bridge, was considered to be one of the most important docking places in London in the middle ages. The name means 'queen's harbour' and it was given in honour of Queen Matilda (Henry I's wife), although it is known to have existed several centuries earlier.

St Mary Overie Dock

This small Bankside dock is named for the nearby Cathedral and Collegiate Church of St Saviour and St Mary Overie – Southwark Cathedral for short. It started out as a priory dedicated to the Virgin Mary, with the 'Overie' bit meaning 'over the river' to distinguish it from the various City churches with the same name.

St Katharine Docks

Located near the Tower, St Katharine Docks (two docks known individually as the Western and Eastern Docks) were built by the engineer Thomas Telford in the 1820s. They got their name from a medieval hospital that had previously stood on the site. Founded by Queen Matilda (King Stephen's wife) in 1148, the Royal Hospital and Collegiate Church of St Katharine by the Tower was named for St Catherine, an early Christian martyr who died in Alexandria in 305AD at the orders of the Roman Emperor Maxentius.

St Saviour's Dock

This small dock – located on the south of the Thames at the point where the subterranean River Neckinger meets it – started out in medieval times as the quay for Bermondsey Abbey, which was dedicated to St Saviour – or, as he was better known, Jesus (who is sometimes referred to as Sanctus Salvator, which translates into English as 'Holy Saviour').

Execution Dock

A dock in name only, the gruesome name reflected its purpose – this was the riverside gallows at Wapping where, for several centuries, convicted pirates were executed. The last execution took place in 1830.

London Docks

Built in Wapping in the early 19th century, these docks consisted of a Western Dock and an Eastern Dock, linked by the smaller Tobacco Dock (which was named for the large warehouse built in 1811 for storing tobacco). The complex was named after the London Dock Company, which was established in 1800. The dock now known as Limehouse Basin opened in 1820 and was used to offload cargoes from ships to barges for transportation inland via the Regent's Canal, which was named after the Prince Regent (later King George IV).

Limekiln Dock

This 18th-century dock at Limehouse was named for the lime kilns that were used to make quicklime for building mortar (the name 'Limehouse' is of similar origin, for the kilns were also known as lime oasts).

Surrey Commercial Docks

Located at Rotherhithe, this group of docks dates back to 1697 when the Howland Great Dock was built; it was named after John Howland, a local landowner. By the mid-18th century it was mainly used by Arctic whalers, which led to it being renamed the Greenland Dock; in the 19th century the complex expanded to accommodate trade from places like Canada, Norway and Russia, all of which had new docks named after them. In 1864, the various docks – the only major ones on the south bank of the Thames – amalgamated under the collective name of the Surrey Commercial Docks.

Millwall Dock

An L-shaped dock in two parts – the Outer Dock runs from east to west and the Inner Dock from south to north – Millwall Dock opened in 1868. Located south of the West India Docks, it was named for the area in which it is situated; Millwall got its name from the mills which stood on the marsh wall in the 17th and 18th centuries.

West India Docks

These three docks on the northern part of the Isle of Dogs were named not for trade from India but from the West Indies. The use of the term 'West Indies' to refer to the Caribbean (as opposed to the 'East Indies', which meant India) dates back to Columbus and came to be used by all of the European powers that acquired islands in that region. The first two docks were built between 1800 and 1802; ships unloaded at the Import Dock (the northernmost of the two) and then loaded up at the Export Dock (later renamed the Middle Dock when a third dock to the south was built).

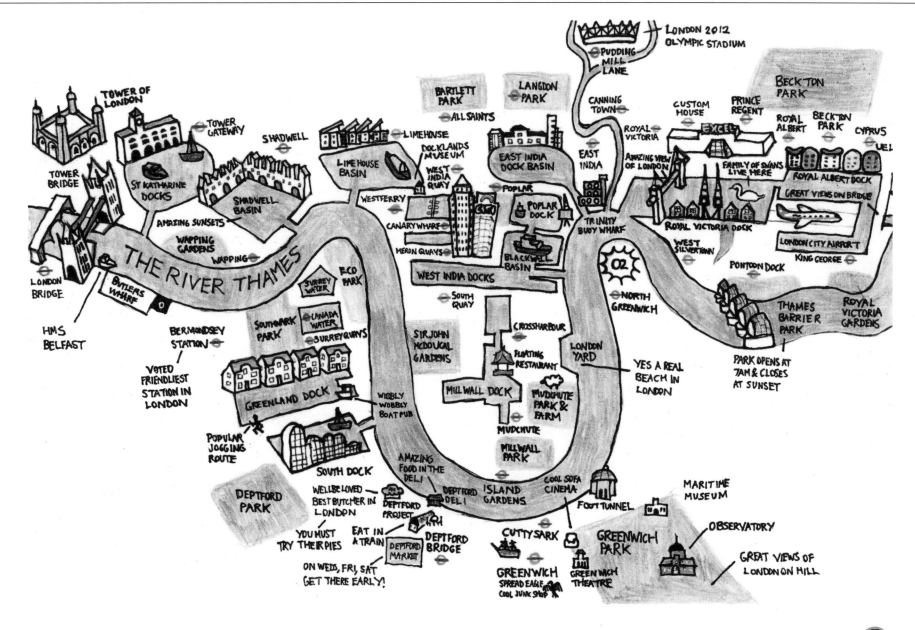

Poplar Dock

Connected to but distinct from the West India Docks, this early 19th-century dock was one of the first to have railway access, and (uniquely) ended up being run by British Rail rather than the Port of London Authority. It got its name from the surrounding area, which in turn was named for the trees which once thrived in the area.

East India Docks

Located in Blackwall, these docks were built in the early 19th century to handle trade from India, and turned a profit through imports of spices, silk, Persian carpets and – most of all – tea. They were built by, and named after, the mighty East India Company, founded in 1600.

Royal Group of Docks

The biggest of London's docks, these were built between 1855 and 1921 in East Ham and West Ham. Not to be confused with the Royal Dockyards (the name given to harbour facilities used by the Royal Navy), they are so-called because they were named after royal personages – the three docks opened in 1855, 1880 and 1921 and were named (respectively) after Queen Victoria, Prince Albert and King George V; a fourth was planned but never built.

Tilbury Docks

Although not located in London, this Essex port has long been a part of the story of London's docks. Located on the Thames Estuary some 26 miles downriver from the Tower, Tilbury has been home to docks since work began in 1882 on a dock intended to rival the (then-new) Royal Albert Dock.

Tilbury greatly expanded in the early 20th century, becoming a large passenger port and later adapting to suit container shipping – it's now one of Britain's three major container ports (along with Felixstowe and Southampton). The name, written as 'Tilberia' in the Domesday Book, means the stronghold (*burh*) of an otherwise unknown person called Tila.

ABOUT THE MAP

Not all of London's docks made it onto Luke Agbaimoni's pen-and-pencil rendition of the Docklands area, but we spot a few of them. We love his annotations as well – a real beach in London?

WHAT LIVES IN THE THAMES?

Spend your days criss-crossing the Thames via various bridges, but never stopped to contemplate what lies beneath? Despite its murky brown appearance, the water quality of the Thames has steadily improved since sewers were repaired in the 1960s, and it is home to seals, otter and even (maybe) seahorses.

Map by
REBECCA LEA WILLIAMS

Species of fish

According to Ian Tokelove of the London Wildlife Trust, there are 125 types of fish in the Tidal Thames (from the estuary mouth to Teddington Lock). Ed Randall of the Thames Angler's Conservancy names bream, perch, pike, roach, rudd, dace, ruffe, barbel, native and non-native carp, chub and gudgeon among them.

The once-prevalent salmon is now rare due to overfishing, but is occasionally spotted on Environment Agency camera traps migrating upstream between October and January, such as at Molesey Weir near Hampton Court.

Non-native species such as zander are occasionally spotted around Teddington. In 2010 the now-defunct British Waterways organisation identified it as one of the non-native species most likely to harm native wildlife along rivers in Great Britain.

Sturgeon have been caught occasionally, like the non-native Siberian sturgeon which was caught in the Thames near Dartford in 2013.

Trout are sometimes hooked – sea trout migrate upriver from the estuary to spawn, whereas brown trout tend to stay up the river. The River Wandle, a tributary of the Thames, is a known trout-spawning ground in the Croydon area. Non-native rainbow trout also occur, but have usually escaped from lakes or fish farms.

Non-native Wels catfish are rare but were introduced to the river in the 1930s and persist to this day, occasionally making headlines due to their size. In 2008, Brett Ridley landed a Wels catfish on the Kingston stretch of the river, believed to be the largest fish ever caught in British waters. In 2013, Chiswick RNLI was called to reports of a body on the foreshore in Barnes, which also turned out to be a catfish.

Eels migrate up the River Thames every year between April and October, but face many hazards and obstacles and are regarded as critically endangered. They are usually found close to the estuary, travelling as far as Greenwich.

Other information about record-breaking or rare fish in the Thames is hard to come by. Anglers are notoriously secretive about specimen catches, as publicity may attract too many others and spoil the fishing in a favourite spot. For any potential anglers, it's worth noting that all fishing in England and Wales requires an Environment Agency rod licence.

Other species

In September 2014, it was announced that seal numbers in the Greater Thames Estuary had increased almost back to their natural rates thanks to a conservation project, after being hunted for fur and meat. While they do mainly hang around in the estuary, we're told that they've been seen as far west as Teddington Lock.

Famously, in 2006, a Northern Bottlenose Whale swam up the Thames until becoming stranded near Battersea and sadly not surviving. It is now in the National Research Collection at the Natural History Museum.

In 2013, a pod of porpoises was spotted near Tower Bridge and a small pod of dolphins was seen in Bermondsey. In 2001 a lone dolphin also made the trip, spotted between Wapping and Blackfriars. Recent improvements in water quality and availability of fish brings these animals to the Thames in search of food. What's the Thames Barrier to stand between a porpoise and its lunch?

Otters are often the hardest to reintroduce to a habitat, so the fact that sightings are on the up (one was spotted on the River Lee a few years back, and they are approaching the western boundaries of the Thames catchment), shows that the waters are once again in excellent health, providing plenty of fish for Tarka and co. to get stuck in to. However, buildings, walls and roads create barriers that they cannot currently get around, accounting for why they are often seen in urban Thames areas.

In 2011, a rare seahorse from the Canary Islands and the Mediterranean was found at Greenwich, leading to theories that a breeding population existed in the Thames.

Pipistrelle and Daubenton's bats will feed over bodies of water such as the Thames, but can be difficult to spot. We recommend signing up for a bat walk which uses electronic bat detectors to track them down.

Where there are fish, there are birds, so a few species to keep an eye out for are swans, grey herons, cormorants, Canada and Egyptian Geese, mallard, grey wagtails and pied wagtails. London Wildlife Trust's Species Explorer has photos of each bird to help with identification – and could be great to keep the kids occupied on a riverside walk.

ABOUT THE MAP

'Investigating the history of London's many rivers and canals for this map opened up a whole new territory for me to explore. The underground or 'lost' rivers of London and the (man-made) canals and navigations all link up to the main overland rivers feeding into the Thames (some smaller tributaries have been left out to avoid overcrowding). Together these make up the London waterways network. I was really taken aback by the vast number of species the Thames hosts. Many of the Thames' tributaries have been 'rewilded', increasing biodiversity – I tried to showcase the variation that can be found.'
- Rebecca Lea Williams

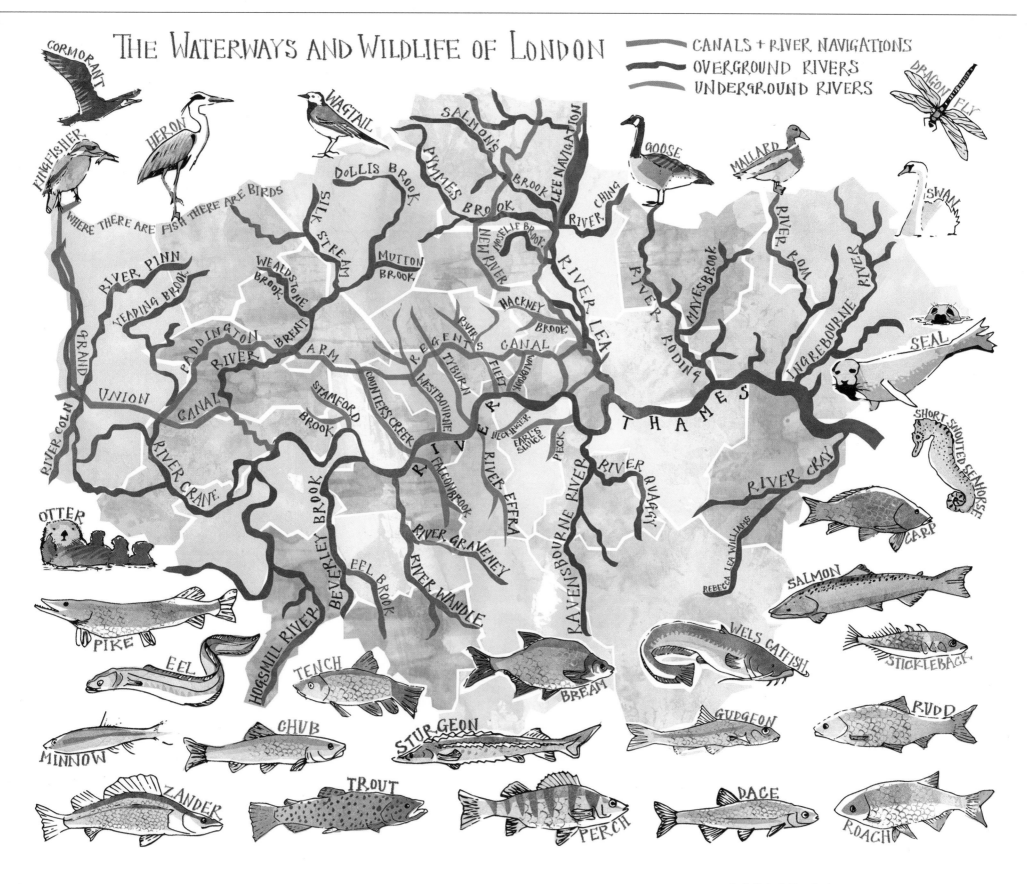

THE WATERWAYS AND WILDLIFE OF LONDON

CANALS + RIVER NAVIGATIONS
OVERGROUND RIVERS
UNDERGROUND RIVERS

CORMORANT

DRAGONFLY

KINGFISHER

HERON

WAGTAIL

GOOSE

MALLARD

SWAN

WHERE THERE ARE FISH THERE ARE BIRDS

SALMON'S BROOK

DOLLIS BROOK

PYMMES BROOK

LEE NAVIGATION

PYMMES BROOK

CHING RIVER

SILK STREAM

MUTTON BROOK

MOSELLE BROOK

NEW RIVER

RIVER PINN

WEALDSTONE BROOK

HACKNEY BROOK

RIVER LEA

RIVER RODING

MAYESBROOK

RIVER ROM

INGREBOURNE RIVER

YEADING BROOK

PADDINGTON

BRENT

RIVER

ARM

REGENT'S CANAL

RIVER

WALBROOK

SEAL

GRAND

UNION

CANAL

RIVER COLN

STAMFORD BROOK

COUNTERS CREEK

TYBURN

WESTBOURNE

FLEET

THAMES

RIVER CRANE

RIVER

FALCONBROOK

RIVER EFFRA

NECKINGER

EARL'S SLUICE

PECK

RAVENSBOURNE RIVER

RIVER QUAGGY

RIVER CRAY

SHORT SNOUTED SEAHORSE

OTTER

BEVERLEY BROOK

EEL BROOK

RIVER GRAVENEY

RIVER WANDLE

REBECCA LEA WILLIAMS

CARP

SALMON

HOGSMILL RIVER

PIKE

EEL

TENCH

BREAM

WELS CATFISH

STICKLEBACK

MINNOW

CHUB

STURGEON

GUDGEON

RUDD

ZANDER

TROUT

PERCH

DACE

ROACH

LONDON'S DECADES OF INVENTION

London has long been a city of innovation. This timeline shows some of the inventions and discoveries over the past 200 years. Some changed the world, some are more whimsical. Note: almost all inventions built on earlier innovations, and most entries here could be challenged by competing claims.

Map by
JULIA FORTE

1991 Wind-up radio: Trevor Bayliss, Eel Pie Island
The serial inventor crafted his most famous gadget after being moved by the AIDS crisis in developing countries. *Also this decade: robotic surgery*

1984 Handheld computer: PSION Organiser
London company PSION has a good claim to selling the world's first pocket computer. Its Organiser and Organiser II blazed a trail for the smartphones most of us carry today. *Also this decade: espresso martini*

1969 Harrier Jump Jet: Hawker Siddeley, Kingston
The famous vertical take-off and landing aircraft had been in development for several years.

1967 Cash machine: Barclays Bank in Enfield Town
The first ATM was unveiled by actor Reg Varney, famous from *On The Buses*. Its inventor was John Shepherd-Barron. *Also this decade: miniskirt, CT scan*

1955 Automatic electric kettle: Peter Hobbs, Croydon
Hobbs (of Russell Hobbs fame) also built the first coffee percolator in 1952. *Also this decade: DNA structure*

1943 Mulberry Harbour: Hugh Iorys Hughes
Portable harbours to support the Allied invasion of Europe in World War II. The structures were designed and built at various locations, but London's docks made a particularly important contribution. Blitz rubble was used to prepare the construction facilities.

1933 Nuclear chain reaction: Leo Szilard, Russell Square
The Hungarian physicist had an epiphany while crossing the road in Bloomsbury. His daydream ultimately led to the physics behind atomic bombs and nuclear power. *Also this decade: modern tube map, regular TV service*

1928 Penicillin: Alexander Fleming, Paddington
This game-changing antibiotic was discovered by serendipity at St Mary's Hospital. *Also this decade: K2 phone box, television, automatic traffic lights*

1901 Powered vacuum cleaner: Hubert Cecil Booth
Booth was inspired by watching inefficient cleaning systems at St Pancras station. His company was quickly overtaken by Hoover, which is why you don't give your carpet a good boothing.

1898 Neon: William Ramsay, UCL
Ramsay was also the first to isolate argon, helium, krypton and xenon, all from his lab in Bloomsbury.

Also this decade: Dewer's vacuum flask, Marconi's wireless telegraph, Escoffier's Peach Melba and Melba toast

1884 Machine gun: Hiram Maxim, Hatton Garden
Strictly, the first recoil-operated machine gun, but Maxim's weapon went on to revolutionise war, and not in a pretty way. *Also this decade: movie camera*

1878 Microphone: David Edward Hughes, Fitzrovia
Several claimants might be credited with this invention, but Hughes was the first to demonstrate a device to an audience and coined the word microphone. *Also this decade: electrocardiogram, questionnaires, radio waves*

1865 Tuxedo: Henry Poole & Co., Savile Row
The Prince of Wales (later Edward VII) wanted an informal dinner suit. His tailor hit upon what we now call the tuxedo. *Also this decade: public weather forecasts, plastic, underground railway, electromagnetism laws, manual traffic lights*

1856 Purple dye: William Perkin, Cable Street
The colour purple was a rare sight until the second half of the 19th century. 18-year-old William Perkin accidentally made the first useful purple dye from his home in the East End. *Also this decade: Darwin's theory of evolution*

1843 Computer Programme: Ada Lovelace, St James's
Lovelace worked out how to run algorithms on Charles Babbage's mechanical difference engines, and is often called the world's first programmer. *Also this decade: postage stamp, Christmas card and cracker, rubber band, bowler hat*

1831 Dynamo: Michael Faraday
Faraday's insights into the relationship between magnetic fields and electricity led to numerous other applications.

1816 Electric telegraph: Francis Ronalds, Hammersmith
A message sent through eight miles of wire was the first electronic communication in the world. Ronalds offered it freely to the British government, who were not interested.

1807–08 Six chemical elements: Humphry Davy, Royal Institution
Davy was the first to isolate sodium and potassium, barium, calcium, magnesium and boron (the latter jointly with others). *Also this decade: pie chart, passenger train*

And earlier: 1786 bar chart; 1770 bristled toothbrush, 1766 jigsaw puzzle, 1723 fire extinguisher…

ABOUT THE MAP

This map takes as its theme London inventions and 'firsts'. Its creator, Julia Forte, is something of a London aficionado. Her map includes such notable human achievements as the world's first oxtail soup and Wellington boots alongside better-known events such as the first television broadcast and first police force. We suspect, like our own list, some of these 'firsts' might be the subject of some dispute, but we love her style – and there's no denying London's innovative spirit.

London firsts

PADDINGTON ①

SHOREDITCH ⑤

OXFORD ST

HIGH HOLBORN

LIVERPOOL ST ②

BERWICK ST ⑲

SOHO ⑱

⑰

COVENT GARDEN

FRITH ST

BOW STREET ⑮

⑯

RING RING ⑳

⑳

PICCADILLY

⑭

⑬

ST JAMES ②②

REGENT ST

TRAFALGAR SQUARE

②③

②④

WESTMINSTER

BIG BEN

WESTMINSTER BRIDGE

St Martin Le Grand ③

MUSEUM OF LONDON ⑨

BISHOPSGATE ④

SPITAL FIELDS

⑥

OLD BAILEY

ST PAULS ⑩

ALDWYCH

FLEET ST

⑪

⑫

STRAND

②⑤

TUDOR ST

BLACKFRIARS

CANNON ST

CORNHILL

⑧

⑦

MONUMENT

LONDON BRIDGE

LOWER THAMES ST

THE TOWER ②⑧

SOUTHWARK BRIDGE

T H A M E S

TATE MODERN

THE GLOBE ②⑥

SOUTHWARK

②⑦

TOWER BRIDGE

WAPPING ②⑨

① WORLD'S 1ST UNDERGROUND TRAINS 1863
② WORLD'S 1ST PUBLIC SHOWING OF A FEATURE LENGTH FILM 1924
③ LONDON'S 1ST PILLAR BOX 1855 ⑤ 1ST PRINTING OF COMMUNIST MANIFESTO 1847
④ LONDON'S 1ST THEATRE 1574 ⑥ 1ST CREATION OF OXTAIL SOUP 1600'S
⑦ LONDON'S 1ST COFFEE SHOP 1652 ⑧ WORLD'S 1ST UNDERGROUND PUBLIC LOO 1855
④ LONDON'S 1ST HOT CHOCOLATE SHOP 1657 ⑩ UK'S 1ST STATE LOTTERY - ST PAULS 1569
⑪ DAILY COURANT - UK'S 1ST DAILY PAPER 1702 ⑫ LONDON'S 1ST HACKNEY CARRIAGE STAND 1634 ⑬ BRITAIN'S 1ST TEA SHOP 1717 ⑭ JOHN BARRETT CREATED THE CELLO 1720
⑮ BOW STREET RUNNERS BECOME 1ST PAID POLICE FORCE IN THE UK 1750 ⑯ UK'S FIRST PUNCH + JUDY SHOW 1662 ⑦ THE EARL OF SANDWICH CREATED THE FIRST SANDWICH 1762
⑱ WORLD'S FIRST TELEVISION BROADCAST, JOHN LOGIE BAIRD 1926 ⑲ FIRST GRAPEFRUITS ARE BROUGHT TO THE UK 1890 ⑳ BELL MAKES THE 1ST LONG DISTANCE TELEPHONE CALL 1876
㉑ LONDON'S FIRST TELEPHONE BOX K2, IS PARKED AT THE ROYAL ACADEMY 1926 ㉒ THE WELLINGTON BOOT WAS INVENTED IN ST JAMES IN THE 1800'S ㉓ JAMES PUCKLE INVENTED THE MACHINE GUN 1718
㉔ MOZART PLAYED HIS 1ST SYMPHONY IN EBURY ST AGED 8 1765 ㉕ THE UK'S 1ST ELECTRIC STREET LAMP 1878 ㉖ WORLD'S 1ST SIGNAL BOX 1836 ㉗ POSSIBLY ONE OF LONDON'S 1ST INNS - TABARD - 1309
㉘ THE FIRST INDOOR LATRINE 1240 ㉙ UK'S FIRST FUSCHIA 1800'S

WHY BRITAIN SETS ITS CLOCKS TO LONDON

Time is a complicated matter. Everyone knows about time difference between Britain and distant nations; most of mainland Europe's ahead, America is behind, but there are differences in time no matter how small the distance between the two places measured.

Map by
HARTWIG BRAUN

For example: the sun rises in Greenwich a whole 23 seconds before one can see it at St Paul's. So why does the whole of Britain set its clock to London, and even more specifically Greenwich?

Mean Time

Greenwich Mean Time originates in the British Observatory, which is based there. They were constantly using science to try to increase their time-keeping accuracy, so became an authority on the subject. This led to the entirety of London surrendering to Greenwich. But the rest of the country wasn't quite so simple.

In the early Victorian period people measured time based on where they were. The clock on Bristol's Corn Exchange is proof of this. An uninitiated passer-by might be a little confused as to why the clock has two minute hands roughly 10 minutes apart. Well, the red hand is set to GMT while the black hand depicts Bristol time – that's time calculated from Bristol's exact longitudinal position.

So why did things change?

In the end, it came down to the railways. As anyone involved with the railways will tell you, time is very important when it comes to trains. This became ridiculously complicated when trains travelled between towns in (marginally) different time zones. Passengers missed trains and – more worryingly – there were a number of trains nearly crashing. In 1847, Great Western Railway put an end to this madness by imposing one unified 'railway time' across their network.

Railway time was set to Greenwich Mean Time, but not everyone took this lying down. The Dean of Exeter was an aggrieved party who for years refused to change Exeter Cathedral's clock from what some viewed as 'the correct time'. Hence the introduction of clocks with two minute hands across the country as a compromise.

After years of the nation informally moving towards Greenwich Mean Time, it became law in 1880 through the Statutes (Definition of Time) Act. Finally the kerfuffle was over and an entire nation was forced to yield to the power of the mighty Greenwich. Be it correct or not.

Keeping the time

Turning to Greenwich itself, the most unusual feature of Greenwich's Shepherd Gate Clock is that it has a 24-hour dial. Mounted on the wall outside the Royal Observatory, it is thought to have been the first clock to display Greenwich Mean Time to the public (although, to this day, it doesn't display daylight saving time). It was originally controlled by electric pulses from a master clock inside the building, but the master clock is no longer in use and this one is controlled by a quartz mechanism. Shepherd refers to Charles Shepherd Junior, who made and installed the clock in 1852.

The Greenwich time ball is perhaps the most viewed object at the observatory; you can see it perched on Flamsteed House without going anywhere near the hilltop complex. Indeed, that's the point. The ball was constructed as an aid to timekeeping for ships on the Thames. Exactly on the hour, as measured by the accurate clocks of the observatory, the ball would be dropped down its support. Ships setting out to sea could then adjust their chronometers to the correct time. The ball was crafted from metal and wood in 1833 by Maudslay, Sons & Field. Originally, the ball was winched up and released by hand. In 1852 the release was automated via an electric impulse from the Shepherd Master Clock. Since the 1950s, the timing has been controlled by a super-accurate clock at the National Physical Laboratory. The ball still drops at precisely 1pm every day.

What the observatory's website doesn't mention is that the ball contains several dents put there during renovations – the builders assumed the historic ball was for the skip and started playing football with it.

ABOUT THE MAP

We love Hartwig Braun's characterful 3D creations, which are part map, part landscape illustration. This one focuses on Maritime Greenwich, with the Prime Meridian arcing across the centre – spot the Greenwich time ball on top of the Royal Observatory in the foreground.

BY HARTWIG BRAUN

THINGS YOU MIGHT NOT HAVE DONE NEAR BRICK LANE

So you've eaten a beigel or curry, bought a vintage jacket and learned what a Huguenot is. You're done with Brick Lane, right? Hmm. Take a look at some of the lesser-known things to do in the area…

Map by
JANE SMITH

Spitalfields City Farm

A couple of minutes walk east of Brick Lane is Spitalfields City Farm. It's free to visit (although donations are always appreciated) and is home to the likes of donkeys, sheep and pigs, all waiting to be stroked/have funny noises made at them. The farm also hosts the annual Goat Race, a pun on the Oxford/Cambridge boat race that got out of hand.

As well as a place to get your dose of cute, Spitalfields City Farm is a working farm. A vegetable garden is run by volunteers, and the wildlife garden attracts different species all year round. There's a small cafe – with queues a lot shorter than those at Beigel Bake.

Shoreditch Nomadic Community Garden

If the City Farm hasn't satiated your appetite for the city countryside, Shoreditch Nomadic Community Garden weds urban with nature seamlessly. It was set up in 2015 to give local people somewhere to grow vegetables – also making use of what was essentially a disused building site. Think large wooden planters meets street art, with occasional special events thrown in. Though locals are in charge of growing things, everyone's welcome to visit.

19 Princelet Street

West of Brick Lane is the tourist spot of Spitalfields Market – between the two sits 19 Princelet Street, a former synagogue telling the stories of refugees to the area, and functioning as a museum of immigration.

The house was built by Huguenots in the 1700s, and has since been inhabited by Irish, Polish and Jewish families. The exhibition describes these waves of people who made Spitalfields what it is today. 19 Princelet Street only opens to the public occasionally: check the website (19princeletstreet.org.uk).

Charles Booth Walks

One of the best East End walking tours you'll go on. Sean Patterson takes you back to the Whitechapel known and mapped by the social reformer Charles Booth. This tour isn't stuck in the Victorian age though: find out where Gilbert and George live, discover the only building in London that's been a church, synagogue and mosque, and learn why Brick Lane is called Brick Lane (charlesboothwalks.com).

Close-Up Cinema

The Brick Lane area is a treat for cinema lovers. You've got Rich Mix showing new releases (it's worth checking out Rich Mix's exhibition and live music programme too), and the nearby Electric Cinema for those who like their films with a little more luxury.

Lesser-known is Close-Up Cinema, a cinema and library dedicated to all things film, and tucked away on Sclater Street. The programme of film screenings is curated to reflect the history of cinema, featuring both reel-to-reel and digital projections. Real film buffs, though, will be drawn to the library and archive, which has more than 19,000 titles – they range from early cinema to independent films, as well as books and publications about the film industry. There's an on-site cafe and bar to boot.

Learn how to make something

You've probably heard of perspex jewellery wizards Tatty Devine, but did you know that the Brick Lane store offers jewellery-making workshops? Spend half a day getting to grips with the tools and techniques the Tatty Devine guys use in creating their products, and take your finished masterpiece home with you.

ABOUT THE MAP

Brick Lane is so packed with fascinating places that it was impossible for us to fit them all in, but local illustrator Jane Smith, who knows the area, has managed to find space for quite a few. Brick Lane doesn't run East–West of course, but from North–South – not the most convenient format for a landscape book. Try turning it on its side if it bothers you.

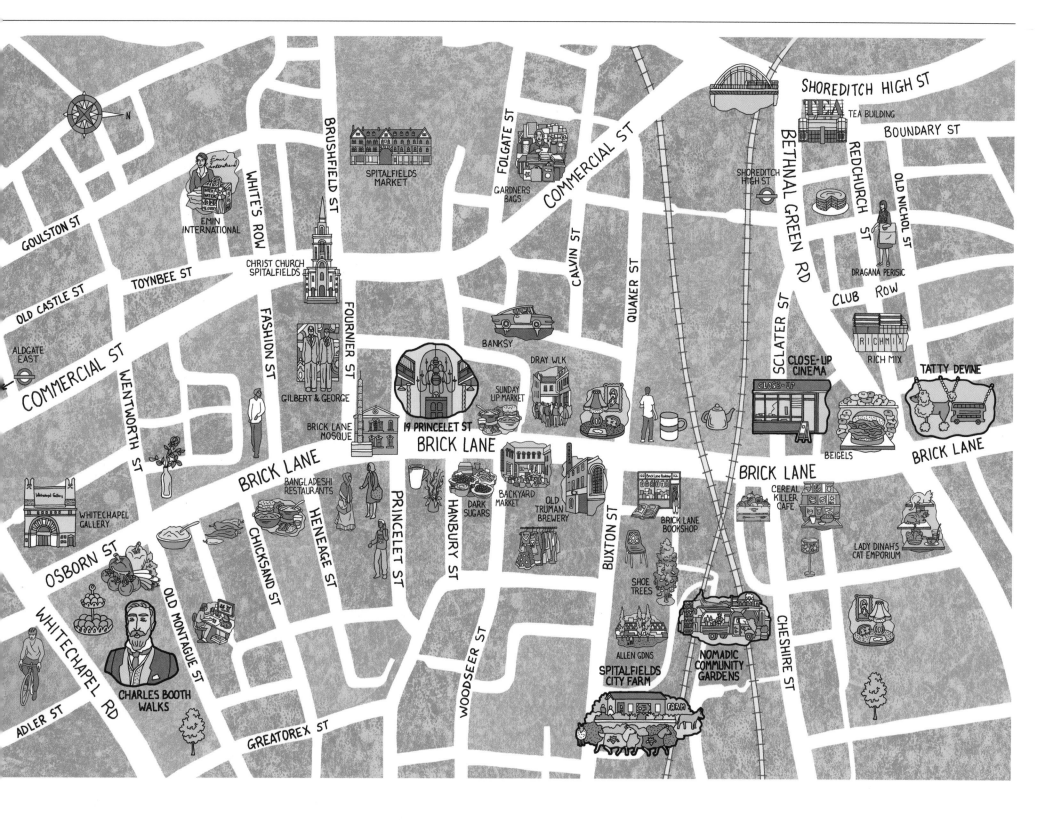

GOULSTON ST

WHITE'S ROW

EMIN INTERNATIONAL

BRUSHFIELD ST

SPITALFIELDS MARKET

FOLGATE ST

GARDNERS BAGS

COMMERCIAL ST

SHOREDITCH HIGH ST

TEA BUILDING

BOUNDARY ST

SHOREDITCH HIGH ST

BETHNAL GREEN RD

REDCHURCH ST

OLD NICHOL ST

TOYNBEE ST

CHRIST CHURCH SPITALFIELDS

FOURNIER ST

CALVIN ST

QUAKER ST

DRAGANA PERISIC

CLUB ROW

OLD CASTLE ST

FASHION ST

GILBERT & GEORGE

BANKSY

DRAY WLK

SUNDAY UP MARKET

SCLATER ST

CLOSE-UP CINEMA

RICH MIX

TATTY DEVINE

ALDGATE EAST

COMMERCIAL ST

WENTWORTH ST

BRICK LANE MOSQUE

19 PRINCELET ST

BRICK LANE

CLOSE-UP

BEIGELS

BRICK LANE

WHITECHAPEL GALLERY

BRICK LANE

BANGLADESHI RESTAURANTS

PRINCELET ST

HENEAGE ST

DARK SUGARS

HANBURY ST

BACKYARD MARKET

OLD TRUMAN BREWERY

BUXTON ST

BRICK LANE BOOKSHOP

BRICK LANE

CEREAL KILLER CAFE

LADY DINAH'S CAT EMPORIUM

OSBORN ST

CHICKSAND ST

WHITECHAPEL GALLERY

OLD MONTAGUE ST

WOODSEER ST

SHOE TREES

ALLEN GDNS

CHESHIRE ST

CHARLES BOOTH WALKS

WHITECHAPEL RD

SPITALFIELDS CITY FARM

NOMADIC COMMUNITY GARDENS

ADLER ST

GREATOREX ST

FARM

LONDON SUBTERRANEA: HOW DEEP DOES LONDON GO?

There's an old and apocryphal London saying that you're never more than six feet away from a rat. This incredible map from Stephen Walter shows how you're never more than a furlong from a subterranean oddity.

ABOUT THE MAP

Like his famed 2008 work The Island, *to which this is a companion piece,* London Subterranea *is a mesmerising tagliatella, combining painstaking research with artistic whimsy. It's too large for us to show the whole thing here, sadly, but we can give you a taste.*

Walter has painstakingly charted the buried rivers, tube lines, bunkers, sewers, government tunnels and other hypogeal secrets of London. He's also included mysterious and underworld elements, such as unsolved murders, ley lines and pagan burial sites.

But just how deep does London go?

The tube network is just one of many subterranean spaces in London. With sewers, water pipes, bunkers, basements, and assorted other tunnels, it's a maze down there. We've attempted to list some of these systems, including the still-under-construction Thames Tideway sewer tunnel.

We've opted to state typical depths below surface level (or high-tide level for the Thames foot tunnels). For example, the tube varies greatly in depth, but is typically 24m. The deepest point is below Hampstead Heath at Bull and Bush (where a station was part-built, but never completed), which reaches 67m.

The deepest space in London is the recently completed Lee Tunnel, a relief sewer that slopes down to 80m beneath Beckton.

4m sewers; **5-6m** cut-and-cover Underground, such as the Circle Line, District Line, Hammersmith & City Line and Metropolitan Line; **6m** Whitehall tunnels, such as those beneath the Churchill War Rooms; **15m** Greenwich foot tunnel; **19.5m** Woolwich foot tunnel; **21m** Mail Rail tunnels – you can actually ride through these at the newly opened Postal Museum in Clerkenwell; **23m** Thames Tunnel, built by the Brunels; **24m (down to 67m)** Tube (deep level); **25m (down to 42m)** Crossrail; **30m (down to 66m)** Thames Tideway Tunnel, London's currently in-construction super sewer; **35m (down to 60m)** London Power Tunnels, newly dug tunnels for London's power supply; **36m** Deep level shelters, built during World War II – Clapham Common shelter now houses a subterranean farm; **40m (down to 65m)** Water ring main: supplying fresh water to Londoners; **55m** Shard piles; **70m (down to 80m)** Lee Tunnel

Naturally this list is only scratching the surface, so to speak. We've left out several road tunnels, tram tunnels, service tunnels and plenty of bunkers, for the sake of clarity. As for what else there might be, lurking somewhere beneath London's surface – who knows?

Map by
STEPHEN WALTER

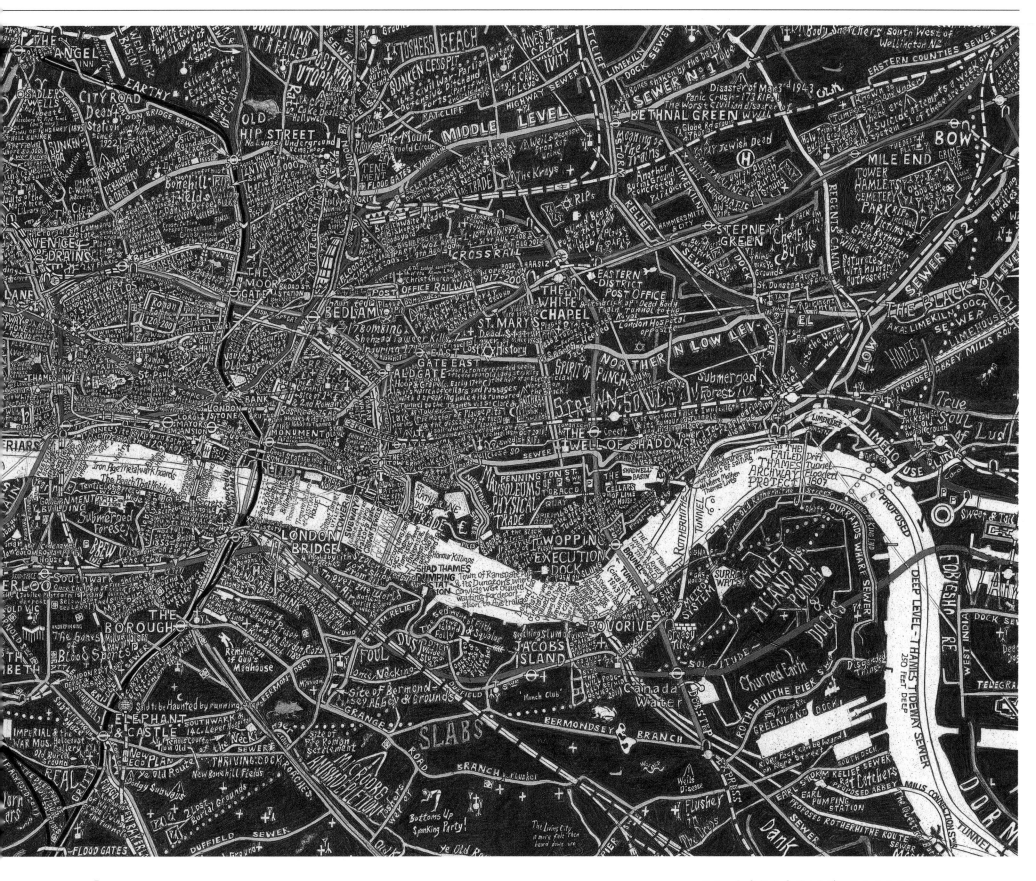

LONDON'S LONGEST ROADS

Did you know that Selfridges is on the same road as the Brecon Beacons? That you can see the Scottish Parliament from a road that passes through Islington? Or that you can walk directly from Lambeth North to Brighton Pier without setting foot on more than one road?

Map by
MATT LANCASHIRE

Then there is the blessed junction outside St Paul's tube station, where roads from two different countries meet. Head west along the A40 (beginning on Newgate) and you'll eventually reach Wales. Choose the northern route past the Museum of London, and you can get into Scotland without leaving the A1.

Welcome to the surprising world of London's A-roads. We tracked a few of the more interesting ones down to their final destinations (with a lot of help from Google Maps and Street View).

The A1: Upper Street to another country
Upper Street in Islington is really badly named. It's actually part of the lower 0.5 per cent of the A1, which stretches all the way up to Edinburgh. This most famous of A-roads begins at St Paul's and travels up Goswell Road past the Museum of London, through Islington and along Holloway and Archway roads and then onwards past Welwyn and Stevenage to the north. Eventually reaching Edinburgh, the final stretches of Britain's longest route adopt the name London Road. **Total length: 410 miles**

The A2: Old Kent Road to Dover
The A2, as Old Kent Road is more prosaically known, begins at Borough tube station as Great Dover Street. It is indeed old and Kentish, forming the southern part of the Roman Watling Street down to Canterbury and Dover. Its London sections pass through New Cross, Deptford and Blackheath before climbing Shooters Hill. There, the A2 dips down into Kidbrooke and Eltham on modern roads, but you can still follow the original Roman route by carrying on east on a dead-straight line through Welling and Crayford (A207). The two routes recombine near Bluewater before heading off into deepest Kent. **Total length: 72 miles**

The A3: Take Borough High Street 'til you reach Portsmouth
Instead of heading east at Borough tube, you might instead go south, down the A3, which eventually reaches Portsmouth. Along the way, it is variously known as Borough High Street, Newington Causeway, Kennington Park Road, Clapham High Street, Wandsworth High Street, Kingston Road and much else besides. **Total length: 74 miles**

The A4: Take Fleet Street to Bristol
Call it the A4 and you have an unmemorable traffic route. Call it Fleet Street, Strand, Pall Mall, Piccadilly, Knightsbridge and Brompton Road, and you have some of the most famous streets in the world. This most notable of roads also comprises Cromwell Road (home of the V&A and Natural History Museum), the embattled Hammersmith Flyover, and the Great West Road before heading out to Bath and Bristol, flirting – and occasionally co-mingling – with the M4. **Total length: 130 miles**

The A5: Edgware Road to Anglesey
Edgware Road and its northern continuations are perhaps the most obviously Roman route in London, heading in a perfectly straight line – save for an Elstree kink – all the way out beyond the M25. This is the northern stretch of Watling Street, the Anglo-Saxon name for the old Roman route out to the Welsh borders. Today, as the A5, it ventures as far as Holyhead in northwest Wales, although it briefly loses its name (becoming the A5183) just outside London. **Total length: 260 miles**

The A10: Take Bishopsgate up to the Norfolk coast
One of the main thoroughfares through the ancient City of London, Bishopsgate formed part of Ermine Street, a Roman road that once led up to York (Eboracum). Sometimes called the Old North Road, it remains one of the straightest roads in London, beginning at Monument station, passing up through Bishopsgate, Shoreditch High Street and Kingsland Road, then on through Dalston, Stokey, Tottenham and Edmonton. Were you to follow the A10 (as it's officially designated) to its conclusion, you'd pass through Cambridge before coming to an end in King's Lynn, Norfolk. **Total length: 106 miles**

The A13: Take Commercial Road out to some Essex mudflats
The A13 leads out from Whitechapel to Southend and Shoeburyness, whisking beachhut-hunting Londoners through many areas of industry and marshy desolation. You'd think there wasn't much more to say about this estuarine highway. You'd be wrong. **Total length: 41 miles**

ABOUT THE MAP

This Mappa Lundi is a particular favourite of ours. According to creator Matt Lancashire, 'I have always believed London is arranged in more of a grid than most people realise. In actually drawing it, I was surprised how many exceptions there were to my griddy rule'. Thanks to its straight lines and major street names it's actually a pretty perfect map to trace some of those routes from our accompanying text as well, although sadly south London isn't included. Next time, Matt?

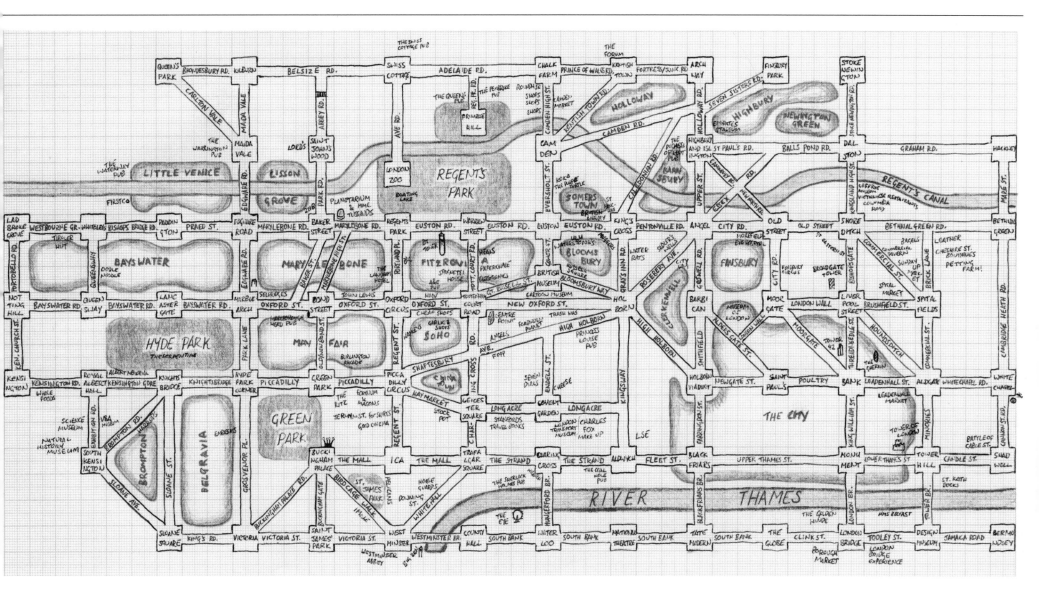

The A23: Kennington Road to Brighton

A single road connects Lambeth North tube station to Brighton Pier. The A23, as it's now known, is another old Roman road, a fact that becomes readily apparent if you follow its largely straight course on a map. Within London, the A23 follows Kennington Road, Brixton Road and Streatham Hill, before heading down through Norbury and Croydon. It then picks up speed by joining the M23 before relaxing back to its A-status on its way down to the coast. **Total length: 52 miles**

The A40: Oxford Street...all the way to Wales

You guessed it, Oxford Street leads to Oxford. But it will also take you to Cheltenham, Gloucester and over the Brecon Beacons to Fishguard in Wales. The stretch known as Oxford Street is about a mile and a half long, although the distance can seem much greater on a Saturday afternoon. This is one of the capital's oldest thoroughfares, following the line of an ancient Roman road that led to Colchester in the east and Hampshire in the west. Today, it's also known as the A40. Within London, it begins just north of St Paul's, runs over Holborn Viaduct and along Holborn, New Oxford Street and Oxford Street, then north to the Westway, Western Avenue, merging briefly with the M40, and thence on to Wales. In days gone by, the A40 took the more satisfyingly straight route of continuing west from Marble Arch along Bayswater Road and Uxbridge Road, running along what is now the A4020. **Total length: 256 miles**

A MICRO GUIDE TO LONDON BOROUGHS

More than fifty years ago, the London Government Act 1963 received Royal Assent. It paved the way, two years later, for radical changes in London's political boundaries.

Map by
ORK INCORPORATED

The 32 boroughs that we still know, love and pay our council tax to date back to just 1965. (The tiny City of London – also known as the Square Mile – holds different political status, and carried on as normal after the Act.) Many former boroughs (Finsbury and St Pancras, for example) disappeared overnight, though you can still see their names on old street signs around town.

What defines a London borough?

The London boroughs as we know them were defined on 1 April in 1965 – the same time as Greater London. Each borough is an area of London that is governed by a local council. There are 32 in total – 12 inner boroughs and 20 outer.

A word about the City of London

The City of London is tiny; just 8,700 people live here. But the City of London isn't technically a borough at all, although it's often lumped in with the rest of them. It's actually governed by the City of London Corporation rather than having its own borough council.

Which is London's smallest borough?

As you might expect, the smallest borough by population is one that's in inner London. Kensington & Chelsea has just 158,000 residents (approximately). This could have something to do with the fact that the current average property price in the borough is just shy of £2m.

How about outer London?

Kingston upon Thames is easily the smallest borough in outer London by population with just 177,000 residents. All other outer London boroughs apart from Richmond (197,000) have a population of more than 200,000.

But what about by area?

Kensington & Chelsea wins this one, too. The entire borough covers just over 7.5 miles, or 12km. Though it's the neighbouring borough of Westminster that's home to 10 Hyde Park Place – arguably London's smallest house – measuring only three feet across.

And the largest?

Croydon and Barnet are the largest two by population – both in excess of 385,000. Croydon also claims to have the largest number of young people of any London borough, which is a nice statistic.

Which borough is growing at the slowest rate?

Increased population size of London has been a topic up for discussion recently and it's actually Kensington & Chelsea that's growing the slowest – its population is expected to increase just 2.1% in the next 10 years to 2026. That doesn't sound all that slow but to put it into context Tower Hamlets is top of the list, with population growth estimated at a whopping 20%.

Which borough has most space then?

It's actually Bromley, the largest of all boroughs by area, that's the least crowded borough – just 2,020 people per square kilometre. It might be sparsely populated, but the calibre of its residents is high: David Bowie, Charles Darwin and H G Wells have all lived in the area.

And which is London's busiest borough?

Duh, obviously Westminster. But we had some fun rooting around in the stats about boroughs' daytime populations from the London Datastore so we thought we'd share.

Westminster has 897,293 people spending significant amounts of time in it during the day; around 175,000 are tourists, so the next time you end up walking in the road to get past a slow-moving group on your lunch break, remember it's far more likely you're muttering 'bloody tourists' at a fellow Londoner. Perhaps it's the 231,000 Westminster residents who are more entitled to mutter 'bloody commuter' at the rest of us that just work there.

So where do I go to avoid the crowds?

If you want peace and quiet, head to Barking and Dagenham, which has a daytime population of just under 180,000. The other two boroughs with less than 200,000 people during the day are Sutton and Kingston upon Thames.

Other busy boroughs are the City (almost 550,000), Camden (nearly 500,000), Southwark (approx 417,000) and Tower Hamlets (a little under 400,000). Kensington and Chelsea has a daytime population of around 253,000, 55,000 of whom are tourists (though it might feel like more around South Ken) – which makes it quieter than Barnet, Brent, Bromley, Croydon, Ealing, Enfield, Hounslow, Islington, Lambeth, Wandsworth and Hillingdon. Ah, Hillingdon. We were initially surprised by the over 350,000 people it attracts during the day, but then we remembered: Heathrow.

ABOUT THE MAP

We've stretched the definition of 'hand-drawn' a little here – Jenny Beorkrem, like many graphic designers nowadays, works on a computer. We like her bold use of typography here – it can't have been easy getting 'Kensington & Chelsea' or 'Barking & Dagenham' to fit!

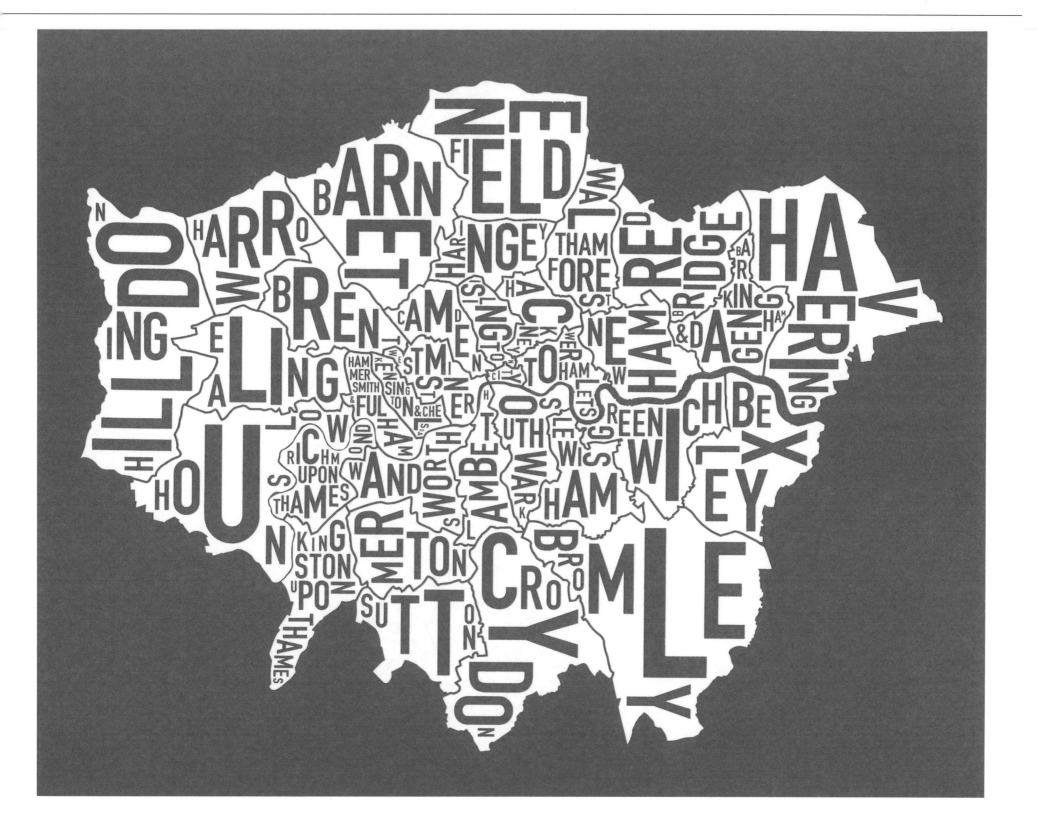

11 TRIVIAL THINGS THAT MAKE LONDONERS REALLY ANGRY

Londoners are an angry bunch, aren't we? We get riled by red lights and infuriated by inanimate objects.

ABOUT THE MAP

In direct contrast to these annals of anger, We Love You London *is a delight. This is Jojo Oldham's own take on the centre of London; she includes 'the best and worst that London has to offer. Full of crap drawings, musings and mistakes.' It's one to savour. 'Bears no resemblance to reality or Google Maps. Please do not try to use it to get anywhere.'*

But are we letting the bile get the better of us when we should just chill out? Here are 11 trivial things which are guaranteed to make a Londoner angry.

1. Eating on the tube
It's funny how the prospect of a fellow passenger chowing down on a sandwich makes us want to break stuff – when did eating on the tube become acceptable? There are a lot of unacceptable things about the tube though; people eating on it is one of the least of them.

2. Sniffing/coughing/throat-clearing
The tube is a dusty, dirty place (and sometimes we're ill as well). Sometimes we need to cough or sneeze or clear our throats of tube dust. We can't help it and we're not doing it to annoy you so get over it and stop glaring at us. But give us a cough sweet first.

3. Bad walking etiquette
This covers a multitude of sins – walking four abreast while dawdling, looking at phones while walking, stopping in the middle of the pavement. Walking and looking at a phone are two mutually incompatible activities yet thousands of Londoners do it every day, seemingly relying on other pedestrians not to walk into them. What's so important that it can't wait till you've sat down somewhere? As for dawdling, anyone who's tried it in Canary Wharf's shopping centre between noon and 2pm will have experienced pedestrian rage – as the old adage goes, never get between a Wharfer and their lunch.

4. Music leakage
We've never quite got how the standard-issue earphones which come with smartphones and MP3 players can be so hopelessly inadequate. Or why our fellow passengers listen to such terrible music. But it infuriates us anyway because it's exactly the kind of noise which isn't loud enough to truly bother us but is just loud enough to be distracting.

5. Not moving down
Whether it's on the train, on the platform or simply in front of the doors, not moving down is guaranteed to rile Londoners. Despite years of posters and daily tannoy reminders telling us to move down, we still congregate around the doors. Part of the reason for this is strategic – stand by the platform exit and you're more likely to get a seat as everyone in that carriage was there precisely because it was by the exit. But it's also down to not wanting to have to force our way back through the crowd of people congregating by the doors to get off the train, otherwise known as a self-fulfilling prophecy.

6. Oyster card unreadiness
Like bad walking etiquette, not having your Oyster card ready for the barriers when you know you need it is trivial in the larger scheme of things but tremendously annoying for the people behind you. The reality is that the hold-up you cause is mere seconds, but we think it might be better to avoid the stress and just have your damn card ready.

7. The cable car
If Boris Johnson had set out to create a stick for his opponents to beat him with, then he couldn't have done better than the cable car. Spending millions in taxpayers' money to build a transport solution which links just two places, only one of which anyone really wants to go to, was never going to win hearts and minds.

8. Leaning on the poles
The poles are for holding, not for leaning. When you lean on the poles, you are preventing someone else from being able to hold it and it's just another of those aggravating things which people with no self-awareness do on public transport. It also means having to break the first rule of public transport which is never to speak to your fellow commuters.

9. Road rage and red lights
Arguably not trivial, but always guaranteed to bring on the red mist. Whether it's cyclists selectively obeying road laws, taxi drivers who see a pedestrian crossing the road then accelerate madly towards them so that they can hoot their horn and make a big fuss, bus drivers blocking pedestrian crossings or traffic lights which only let two cars through, London's roads are one of the angriest places to be.

10. Delays
Anything that holds us up makes us seethe, from delays on the tube to someone paying for a fizzy drink with a debit card.

11. Generally being objectionable
The list of trivial yet irritating behaviour which falls under this heading could be endless. To name but a few – spitting on the pavement, talking loudly on your phone in enclosed spaces, audible gum chewing, boisterous teenagers on the bus, misbehaving toddlers on the tube, people dropping litter, those weird scooter things you see a lot of in Shoreditch, not standing on the right – it just goes on and on.

Map by
Jojo Oldham

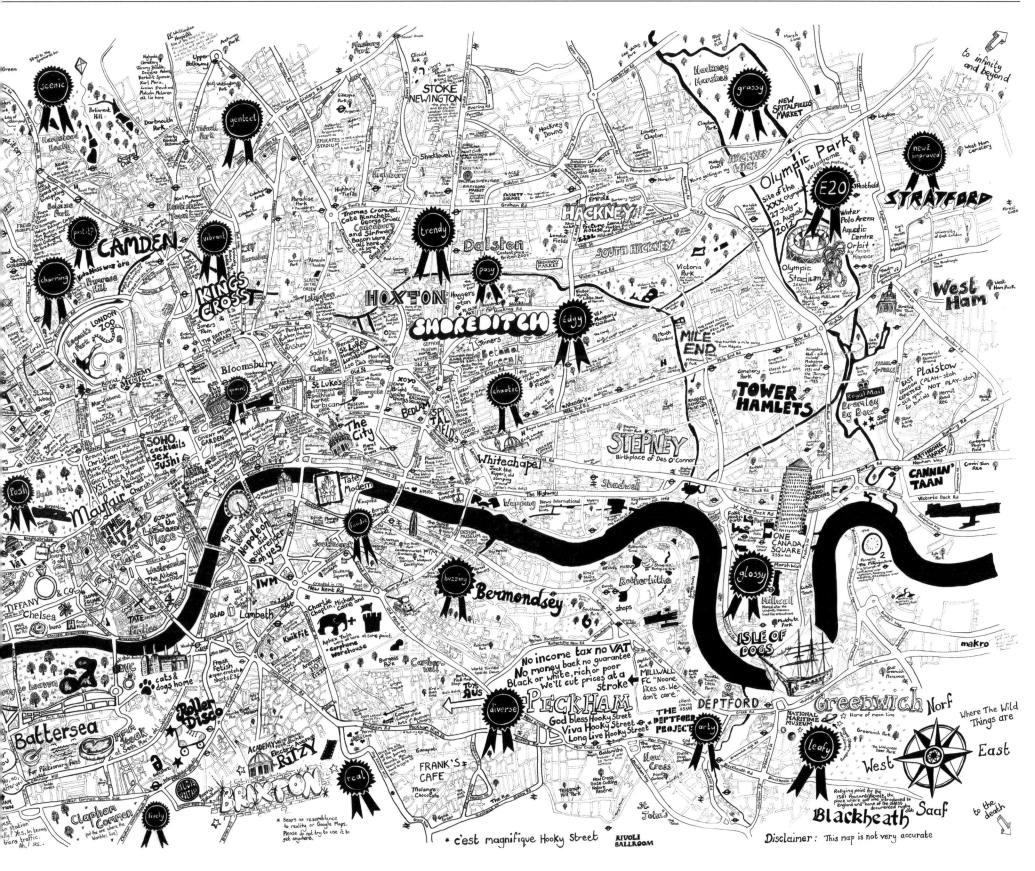

PLACES WHERE LONDON HAS MUSIC IN ITS DNA

London is made up of many different neighbourhoods with their own unique and identifiable character. Sound is often central to this character. Different music genres have flourished across the capital, often finding their true home in one particular area.

Map by
THE LONDON MUSIC MAP

Camden

Despite what you might believe walking Camden's streets today, punk was not born here. It's an import that arrived in a chaotic package in the form of The Ramones on 4 July 1976, at The Roundhouse. The next night, the band visited another Camden venue, Dingwalls. The spark was lit and has burned bright ever since.

Many key members of British punk were at those shows, including The Clash, who shot the cover to their debut album on Camden's backstreets. Members of The Sex Pistols were also in tow for those Ramones shows, and the band would later grace the Dingwalls stage themselves.

Today you'll see many market stalls selling (fake) Sex Pistols merchandise, but it's worth noting that, like punk itself, the band was an import to Camden. The Sex Pistols' beginnings centred on edgy fashion boutiques on Chelsea's King's Road. Ask a Chelsea resident for their interpretation of 'God Save The Queen' and it'll quickly become clear why Camden is a better fit for the band today.

Bow

Grime's made a real comeback in recent years across the whole country, so it's easy to forget the genre's humble beginnings. Ask every grime MC where it all started, and they'll all bring up one name: Wiley. The godfather of grime, as he's affectionately known, is from Bow. His contributions to the scene and the area led to him getting his own paving stone – Wiley himself chose to have it placed outside Bow School, which he attended.

Not only did grime begin in Bow but Wiley's famous protégé Dizzee Rascal, who brought the genre into the mainstream, is also from here. Since then the music has sunk its claws into the entire city.

Soho

Soho's been through many phases in its history. It was once the focal point of the nation's film industry. To many, it immediately conjures up associations of pornography and sex shops. And at one time it was the fulcrum of rock'n'roll in London.

The 2i's Coffee Bar was Europe's first rock'n'roll venue, where acts such as Cliff Richard and Tommy Steele were discovered. From there things only got bigger and better with the opening of The Marquee Club. The likes of The Rolling Stones, Led Zeppelin, The Who, Pink Floyd, David Bowie, Jimi Hendrix and Fleetwood Mac played there, cementing the area as London's rock'n'roll district.

Elephant & Castle

Sipping on a delightful pint inside the Elephant & Castle Pub, you might be unaware that you're in ground zero for UK Garage. In the nineties, the pub hosted a nightclub afterparty named Happy Days every Sunday from 10am–2pm. It attracted punters from nearby mega-club Ministry of Sound, who were still raring to go after that mecca shut at 9am. The DJs were worried that after a night of hard partying the ravers' energy reserves would be running low. So to remedy tiredness, they sped up the records. Combine this with bass so loud that it 'literally shook the windows'.

There was a large outcry in 2015 when it emerged the pub was shutting down to be replaced by that bastion of gentrification, Foxtons estate agents. The plans didn't go anywhere, and instead the pub reopened under its former name.

Notting Hill

Head down to Notting Hill Carnival and you'll hear a swirling cavalcade of genres, but one distinctive sound dominates above all others. Booming out of sound systems across the distinctive part of west London are the sounds of reggae and dancehall.

The carnival is a celebration for Britain's Caribbean diaspora, so with it comes their music. Everyone is charmed by Europe's largest street festival.

Peckham

Everyone knows how 'cool' and 'trendy' Peckham is right now, but it wasn't always this way. How did it change from Del Boy's locale to that of Wavey Garms? Soul music played a large part in attracting today's young people to ride the Overground down from Dalston. The South London Soul Train night – apparently the world's largest soul night, sprawling across multiple floors – at the area's epicentre The Bussey Building started this. Since then the music and clothing label Peckham Soul has launched in an attempt to cement Peckham as London's soul town.

ABOUT THE MAP

The London Music Map is the creation of music producer Nick Faber, who had the idea for a map of London music sites when walking around the city thinking about all the famous locations where classic music has been created over the years. Says Nick: 'If you didn't live here or didn't know where they were, you might walk past a lot of these legendary locations. I wanted to get as many of them down on a map so people could discover them for themselves.' It's illustrated by graphic artists RUDE, and even has its own website.

WHEN WARDOUR STREET WAS 'FILM ROW'

Walk down Soho's Wardour Street today and you'll notice plenty of bars and restaurants of all different pedigrees alongside a few post-production houses, and other fairly anonymous West End office spaces. Look a little closer, however, and you can find some clues as to the street's relatively uncelebrated past as London's 'Film Row.'

Map by
DEX @ RUN FOR THE HILLS

Charles Urban: Trendsetter

The first film company to set up business in Wardour Street belonged to Charles Urban.

On 1 May 1908, Urban moved into 89–91 Wardour Street, calling the building Urbanora House. Two years later, his business was expanding, taking over the building on the other side of the street (numbers 80–82), and calling it Kinemacolor House in honour of his ground-breaking new colour-film company.

Where Urban led, others followed; even some foreign film companies looking for London headquarters moved into the street. By 1914, Wardour Street housed more than 20 film companies, including British Pathé (next door to Urban at 84, and also at 103–109).

Flammable Film

The successful but short-lived Ideal film company moved into the premises at 76–78 Wardour Street just before World War I. In his memoirs, the co-founder Harry Rowson recalls how the stores of extremely flammable celluloid film stock meant the price of insurance for London film companies was especially high.

As a result, film dealers looked for buildings with low rents, away from the usual business districts. There was also an incentive to share premises, in order to save on costs. Rowson's company paid £650 a year to lease the ground floor and basement of 'a modern fire-proof building' on the corner of Meard Street, formerly occupied by printers. 'I thought it the most conspicuous film office in London at that time, situated in the heart of theatreland,' said Rowson.

By 1926, there were around 40 film companies on Wardour Street. The nearby Shaftesbury Avenue, Gerrard Street and Charing Cross Road also housed plenty of film companies. In 1929, the old Faraday Electrical Works at 146–150 had been rebuilt as the modern-style office building Film House.

Welcoming Warner Brothers and Hammer Productions

Warner Brothers opened an office and film store at 135–141 Wardour Street in the 1930s, as did J Arthur Rank, British industrialist and owner of the Rank Organisation British entertainment conglomerate. You name it, they did it: make films, run studios, own cinemas, sell radios and so on. National House, at 60–66 Wardour Street, was occupied from May 1935 by a new film distribution company called Exclusive Films. Exclusive Films was run by a comedian and businessman called William Hinds in conjunction with a a former cinema owner and Spanish émigré Enrique Carreras.

Earlier, in November 1934, the pair had registered a new film company called Hammer Productions Ltd. The company name came from Hinds' stage name, Will Hammer, which in turn came from the place Hinds called home: Hammersmith. The following years saw bankruptcy and liquidation for Hammer Productions, but Exclusive survived. And by 1949, Hammer was back.

On 12 February of that year, Exclusive registered Hammer Film Productions as a company with Enrique and James Carreras, and William and Tony Hinds as directors. Hammer moved into the Exclusive offices in 113–117 Wardour Street, and the building was rechristened 'Hammer House'. By the late 1950s, the company would dominate the horror market, enjoying international success. It's hard to believe, but by the late 1940s there were around 100 film companies rubbing shoulders along Wardour Street. And by the end of the 20th century, the film companies on Wardour Street had been joined and then replaced by other media firms: TV and video companies, post production houses, and advertising agencies.

Wardour Street Today

Wonder what it's like inside those old Pathé Film offices today? They were converted in 2016 to, guess what: 13 luxury apartments, a gym, and two duplex penthouses.

ABOUT THE MAP

We love themed maps and we love typographic maps, so an illustrator who combines the two was always going to be right up our alley. We're not sure if Dex has seen every single one of the movies depicted in his Central London Film Map, but there should be plenty of ideas here to keep you occupied through a rainy afternoon (or 100). If you make it through the entire map, there's a larger London version available.

THE FORGOTTEN GREAT THEATRES OF LONDON

Throughout Victorian Britain the industrial revolution brought not just widespread employment to the working classes, but labour reform laws that increased safety standards while decreasing working hours. Ordinary working people soon found themselves with the newfound luxury of leisure time. Londoners could attend one of the growing number of theatres that were popping up across London's urban sprawl, particularly in the West End.

Map by **GH BARTLETT**
Originally published by **GEORGE H YOUNG, BOSTON**

We sifted through the old ticket stubs and performance programmes to shine the spotlight on some of the grand old theatres of London that disappeared as the city evolved…

Alhambra

Today many Londoners view Leicester Square as a grimy tourist location that should be avoided at all costs, but it was once the home of the beautiful Alhambra Theatre. With a large domed roof, flanked by two minarets, this opulent Orientalist-style theatre seriously contrasted in size and style with the surrounding structures of Leicester Square. It started life in 1854 as The Royal Panopticon of Science and Arts, which sought to educate its visitors with art exhibitions and live scientific experiments. In 1858, it reopened simply with the aim to entertain. Acts included trapeze artists, variety show singers and risqué performances of the now infamous Can-Can. Indeed, the October 1870 Parisian chorus-line was deemed so sexually provocative that the theatre lost its licence. It was only after a tamer act was discovered – an equestrian ballet, no less – that a new licence was obtained in 1871.

Regardless of scandals, or perhaps because of them (for the theatre's entrance was a notorious location for prostitutes), the theatre remained a popular venue and was even rebuilt following a devastating fire in 1882. During World War I comic musical acts were a favourite with the soldiers on leave. After the war, in February 1925, the theatre held the first live radio broadcast of The Royal Variety Performance, attended by the British royal family. Soon after this date, however, live entertainment was eclipsed by the new technology of cinema, and in 1936 the theatre was demolished to make way for the Odeon Leicester Square, which still stands on the site.

St James's Theatre

The original St James's Theatre was a grand neo-classical building located in the wealthy residential district of St James. Opening in December 1835, it would become an important location in Britain's cultural history for the next 100 years – even Charles Dickens appeared here once, somewhat unexpectedly, as one of the ensemble cast in an amateur performance of Ben Jonson's *Every Man in his Humour*.

By the 1890s, the theatre had become the favourite venue for playwright Oscar Wilde, who used St James's stage to debut *Lady Windermere's Fan*, which premiered in 1892, and *The Importance of Being Earnest* three years later in 1895. It was during the successful run of the latter play that drama occurred outside of the auditorium walls, when the Marquis of Queensbury was forcibly banned from entering the theatre, as it was believed that he was due to insult Wilde by throwing a bouquet of rotting vegetables onto the stage mid-performance. The feud had begun when Wilde became the lover of Queensbury's 25 year-old son, escalating shortly after the event at the theatre into a libel trial that ultimately led to Wilde's imprisonment for sodomy.

The theatre survived the scandal and continued to premiere new works by George Bernard Shaw and even adaptations of Agatha Christie novels. It survived World War II, sustaining only minor damage during a 1944 raid, before coming under the management of Sir Laurence Olivier and his wife Vivien Leigh. These icons of British theatre brought further acclaim to St James's, starring in critically-acclaimed productions while premiering new works by playwrights such as Terence Rattigan.

Despite these successes, the theatre was forced to close in 1957 as the landowner sold the site to a commercial developer. Vivien Leigh fronted a passionate campaign to protect St James's from the wrecking ball. In the post-war fervour to rebuild a modern city, however, the theatre was demolished and replaced by a modern office building.

Strand Music Hall/Gaiety Theatre

A theatre stood on the northeast side of the cross-section between the Strand and Aldwych from 1864 until the 1950s. The Strand Music Hall, as it was originally called, was built on the site of the original Lyceum Theatre, which relocated to its current location just a stone's throw away on Wellington Street (the one showing *The Lion King* ad infinitum).

Four years after opening, the theatre was rebuilt in a much grander style and reopened in December 1868 as The Gaiety Theatre, with performances encompassing pantomime, burlesque and operettas. The Gaiety was an important player in the development of the light-hearted musical comedies that succeeded the music hall genre. It was also particularly famous for the Gaiety Girls chorus line, who appear to be the first generation of female performers to gain social acceptance. They were charming, witty and always dressed in the latest fashions but with modesty that won them much male interest. Many of these actors, in fact, managed to climb the social ladder into the upper class and aristocracy by marrying their wealthy stage-door admirers.

The theatre closed for renovations in the late 1930s but suffered extensive damage during the Blitz and never reopened. The bombed theatre was demolished in the 1950s and a large luxury hotel now fills the sizable space on the corner of Aldwych. Before the Gaiety was torn down, however, some of the auditorium's internal fixtures were mysteriously saved; they now grace the upstairs bar of The Victoria pub near Lancaster Gate tube.

ABOUT THE MAP

This is a section of The Illustrated Map of London or Stranger's Guide to the Public Buildings, Theatres, Music Halls & Places of Interest, *which is quite a mouthful. And no, it's not a modern hand-drawn map; it was published c.1877, and features many charming illustrations, including several places which are either no longer known by these names, or no longer exist at all.*

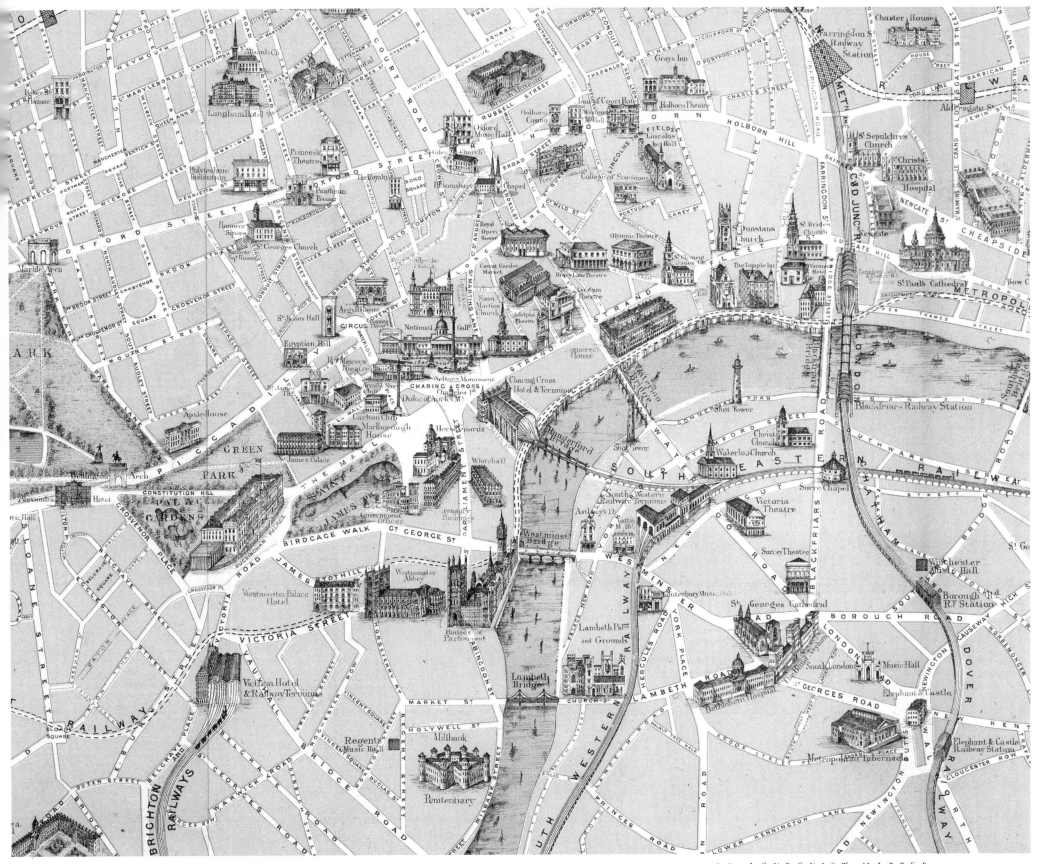

FOUL PLAY: WHEN LONDON BANNED FOOTBALL

Edward II has been called a great many things. 'A good sport' is not one of them.

Map by
KATE ROCHESTER ILLUSTRATION

More than 700 years ago, the King was leant upon by merchants to ban football in London. Down came the edict from the Lord Mayor: ruffians in the city were to cease this 'great noise… caused by hustling over large balls'. The penalty? A suspension to end all suspensions: a stint in one of London's brutal prisons.

Criminal decision, ref

A cruel, hot-tempered game capable of engendering in players and spectators alike the most base, animal passions… and the medieval version wasn't much better. When he'd called foul play, Edward was taking exception not to a beautiful game akin to modern footy, but to mob football: a 'friendly kind of fight… a bloody and murdering practice', as the Puritans would later describe this enduring pastime.

It's possible that football developed independently on this very isle, as a violent contest all but indistinguishable from provincial warfare. (Imagine a time when 'London' meant many rival towns, not yet a unified urban blob). Or it might have been brought over by conquering Roman or Norman soldiers. Either origin would explain the spirit of extreme aggression into which the game was entered.

Injury time

Most local varieties of football were craftily tagged onto a respectable community gathering or religious event, such as Shrovetide. In the lands we now call London, the sport probably witnessed two hordes of combatants, perhaps entire villages, employing any unbroken limb to scramble, boot or chuck a pig's bladder or similar into the opposing horde's goal – some designated monument at the far end of the village like a church, common or pond. Physically the game was closer to rugby, but still utterly lawless.

Because 'teams' numbered hundreds of players, the 'pitch' was a network of narrow streets, sometimes miles long. 'Kit' might include weaponry, 'tactics' might involve burying the ball or simply bludgeoning opposing players, and a match's death toll could exceed its scoreline. Naturally, these melées were the preserve of thrill-seekers. An 1175 account by William FitzStephen recalls packs of adolescents and workers congregating in London's streets. Because each man brought his own ball, the ensuing scenes must have been chaotic indeed, with FitzStephen observing keen elder spectators coming down to 'relive their own youth vicariously'.

The King's 1314 London ban was Britain's first, and inspired at least 30 others – whether it was Edward III encouraging players to switch to archery to stave off the French, Richard II proscribing vulgar ball games generally, or a conflicted Henry VIII hanging up his own football boots (his pair supposedly being the first ever recorded) to instigate his own prohibition.

They didn't think it was all over

But no ban ever stuck. Well, it's the people's game, isn't it? Into the 17th century and beyond, football was still causing a healthy amount of 'disorder and tumult' in London, and for every entry in the Middlesex County Records worrying about this 'great affray likely to result in homicides', there was a 100-strong gang of 'malefactor' enthusiasts in Ruislip who couldn't care less.

Quietly, the game was being civilised. That the London Brewers' Company records of 1421–3 had made reference to a hall booking by a 'fraternity' of footballers has been used to suggest that clubs emerged centuries before the development of organised football. In the 1500s, a London teacher called Richard Mulcaster started thinking up rules for what would be a more genteel sport, overseen by an actual referee, with fixed numbers and positions.

There's little evidence that Mulcaster's rules – or those pioneered in any footy-mad public school over the following centuries – factored into the auspicious 1863 meeting in a Covent Garden pub in which modern association football was born. But they'd worked to make respectable a not-so-harmless but beloved community tradition, which had sustained friendships and hostilities across the city for centuries. And the day London's oldest extant professional club Fulham formed in 1879, the collective soul of SW6 must have thrilled at the memory of boisterous Sundays spent walloping the old pig's bladder at bloomin' Hammersmith.

ABOUT THE MAP

Football isn't London's only sport of course, so Kate Rochester has mapped some of London's biggest sporting venues – rugby, tennis, cricket, and cycling all have their place here, as well as the variety of sports hosted by Queen Elizabeth Olympic Park (including West Ham football club, who now play in the former Olympic stadium), the O2 Arena and Crystal Palace Sports Centre. Even the Thames is a sporting venue, if you count the boat race.

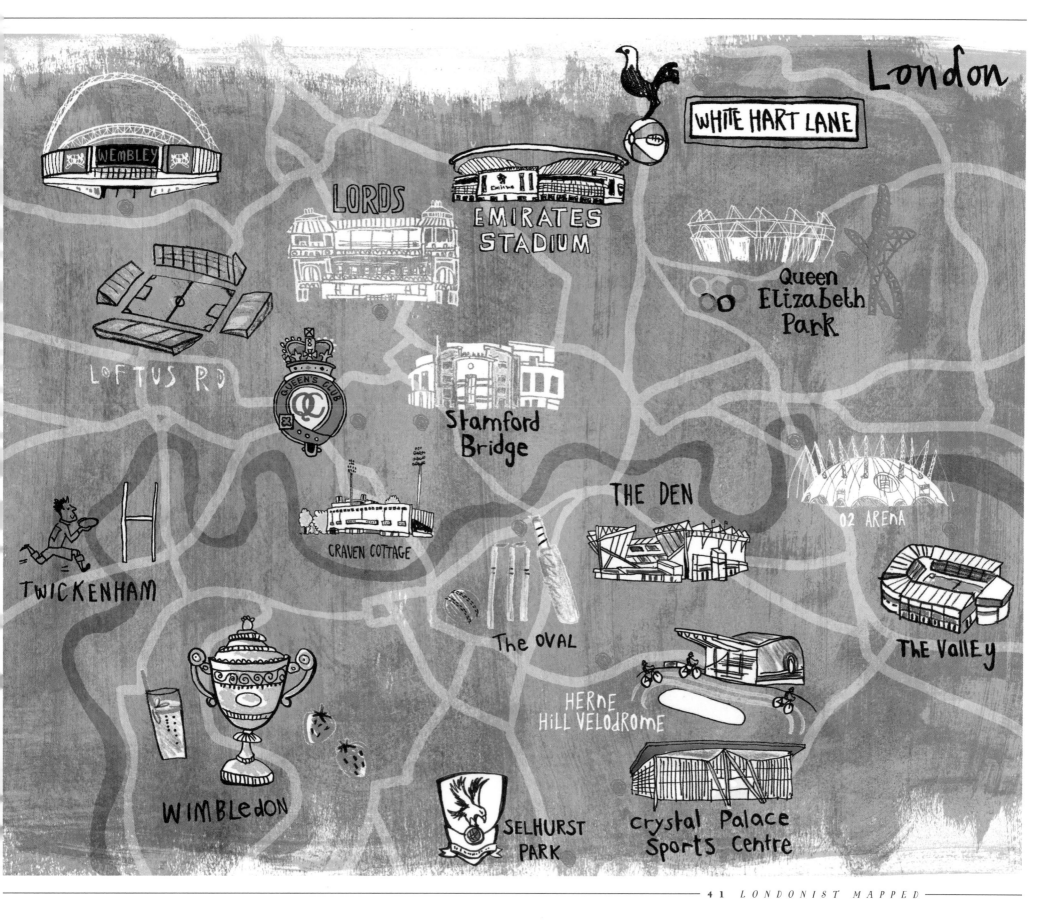

London

WEMBLEY

LORDS

EMIRATES STADIUM

WHITE HART LANE

Queen Elizabeth Park

LOFTUS RD

QUEEN'S CLUB

Stamford Bridge

THE DEN

02 ARENA

TWICKENHAM

CRAVEN COTTAGE

THE VALLEY

The OVAL

HERNE HILL VELODROME

WIMBLEDON

SELHURST PARK

Crystal Palace Sports Centre

LONDON'S BEST LITERARY STATUES

So many books have been written about, or in, London that it's impossible for us to even begin listing them all, so we're not even going to try. Some, though, have left a physical mark on the city – ever made plans to meet someone 'by the Peter Pan statue in Kensington Gardens'? We have.

Map by
DOROTHY

Here's our pick of London's best literary statues, to people (and animals) both real and imagined.

Paddington Bear

One of London's most famous fictional residents, Paddington Bear is immortalised in a bronze statue by Marcus Cornish in Paddington Station. Michael Bond's first book about the bear from darkest Peru was published in 1958, based on a lone teddy bear that Bond saw on a shop shelf near the station. The statue was created in 2000. Give him his due – he heeds National Rail's advice of not leaving his luggage unattended.

Oscar Wilde

Not the most traditional of sculptures, being that it's mostly reminiscent of a coffin-shaped bench, but then Oscar Wilde wasn't a typical kind of guy. His memorial in Charing Cross is officially called *A Conversation with Oscar Wilde*, the idea being that his oh-so-inviting visage entices the passer-by to take a seat and engage the famous playwright in conversation. It took almost a century from Wilde's death in 1900 to get a memorial – the green granite-and-bronze tribute by Maggi Hambling was not unveiled until 1998.

Peter Pan

A bronze Peter Pan statue is located in Kensington Gardens, which author J M Barrie used as inspiration for his tale about the boy who never grew up. Barrie himself commissioned the statue, which was created by Sir George Frampton and unveiled in 1912, 10 years after the first story of Peter Pan was published. The base of the statue is a tree trunk, with rabbits and fairies clambering over it.

John Keats

Poet John Keats has swapped the safety of the 'burbs in Hampstead for – heaven forbid – south of the river. The first statue of Keats was unveiled in Guy's Hospital in 2007 by then-Poet Laureate Andrew Motion. The alcove in which Keats is perched comes from the Old London Bridge (see page 72), so double history points for visiting this site. The bronze cast is by sculptor Stuart Williamson.

Winnie the Pooh

There are actually two statues of Winnie the Pooh at London Zoo (AA Milne's books are inspired by a bear named Winnipeg who used to reside here). One statue shows Winnipeg with Lt Harry Colebourn, the Canadian soldier who gifted her to the zoo; there is also a statue of Winnie the bear alone.

John Betjeman

Many Londoners and tourists in St Pancras International hurry daily past the statue of a man looking up – presumably at a departure board – without knowing much about it. It portrays former Poet Laureate Sir John Betjeman, and was unveiled when the station reopened in 2007. As well as his literary work, Betjeman is credited with helping save St Pancras station from demolition.

Sherlock Holmes

You won't need Watson's help to find the larger-than-life (3m, to be precise) bronze statue of Sherlock Holmes outside Baker Street station, around the corner from his famous 221b Baker Street abode. Sculpted by John Doubleday in 1999, it was funded by the now-defunct Abbey National, whose building was on the site of 221b (the modern-day Sherlock Holmes Museum is actually at 239 Baker Street). There is no statue of Sherlock's creator Sir Arthur Conan Doyle in London, but there is one in Crowborough, East Sussex, where he lived just before his death.

Virginia Woolf

Although Tavistock Square is largely dominated by the Gandhi statue, a bust of Virginia Woolf also resides there – so hard to get A Room of One's Own in London these days. The author wrote many of her books in her former residence on the square. The bust was sculpted from life in 1931, and was moved to its current home in 2004 by the Virginia Woolf Society of Great Britain.

William Shakespeare

Monuments to Shakespeare are plentiful in London, but perhaps the most famous (and certainly the one that gets most passing foot traffic) is the one slap-bang in the middle of Leicester Square. Will was removed briefly for a spit and polish as part of a spring clean of the entire area, but resumed his usual position in Autumn 2013, and has been rueing the arrival of M&M's World to the area ever since.

ABOUT THE MAP

The creators of this charming map (an extract of which is printed here) have taken the names of more than 600 books and arranged them into a street map that bears more than a passing resemblance to London. It's actually based on a turn-of-the-century London street map – we spot Aldwych and the Elephant and Castle roundabout – but, like the best fiction, it's not quite reality.

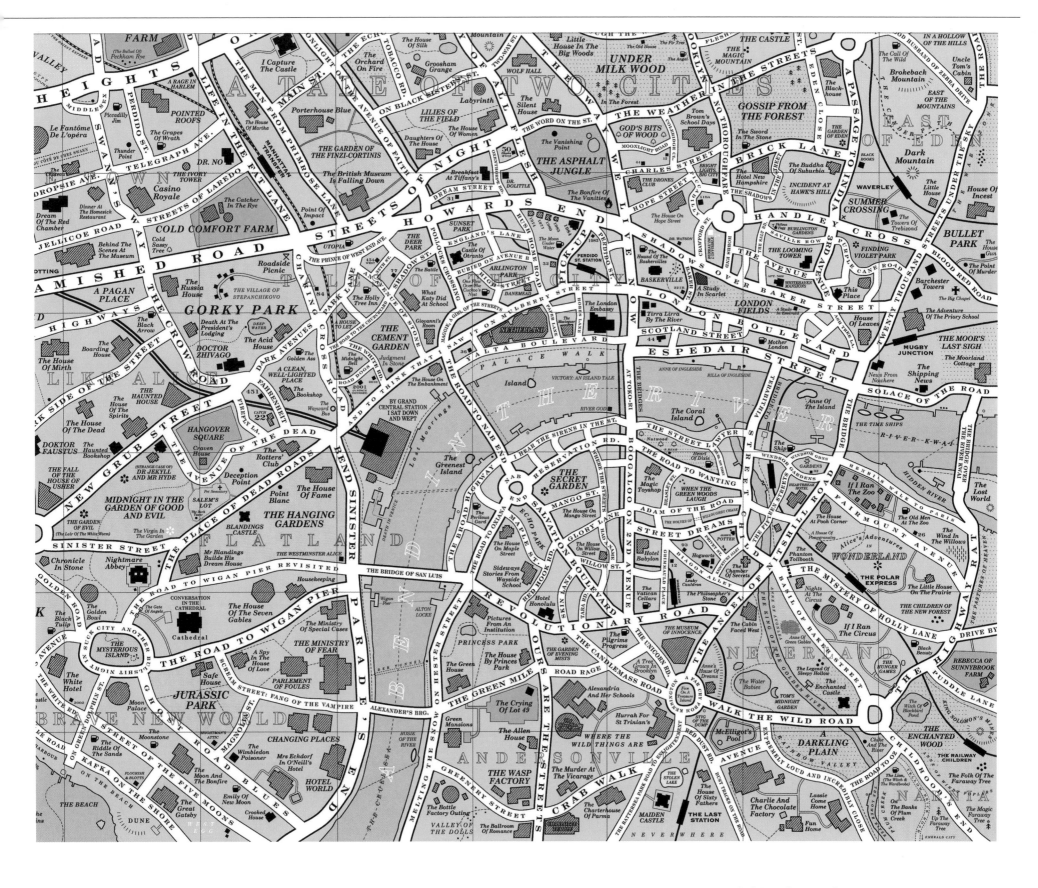

THE LOST LONDON TUBE MAP

Imagine an alternative London, where you can catch a direct tube from Biscuit Town to the Leper Hospital. Where you hop on the Circle at the West London Air Terminal and change at Hippodrome for a train to Bedlam. This is the tube map of Lost London, showing buildings, shops and physical features that were once well known but have now faded into history.

Map by
MARK WATKINSON

Some losses are definitely for the best. Few would welcome back the public horror of Tyburn gallows, or the miserable Marshalsea Prison. Other losses are a cause of some regret. Imagine a city where Whitehall Palace still stands, and Old London Bridge yet straddles the Thames.

Of course, we're barely scratching the surface, and we don't have room to include all the important stuff lost from central London. Below is a potted guide to our chosen lost landmarks.

Aldwych Spur (Holborn): One of London's many lost 'ghost' stations, Aldwych closed to passengers in 1994, along with the short branch of track from Holborn. The station opens for occasional tours.

Angel Inn (Angel): The local tube station, wider area and Monopoly property are named after a now-vanished coaching inn, which occupied the busy crossroads site from the late 16th century. The present building is now a Co-op bank.

Astley's Circus (Waterloo): The world's first circus ring was pioneered close to what is now Waterloo Station. Astley's Circus developed over a succession of increasingly impressive buildings during the late 18th century, and almost made it to the 20th century.

Astoria (Tottenham Court Road): The much-lamented gig venue was swept away in 2009 to make way for Crossrail.

Barkers (High Street Kensington): Kensington's most famous department store lasted from 1870 to 2006. Its most recent building still stands.

Baynard's Castle (Blackfriars): A small fortress near Blackfriars, built not long after the Norman Conquest but demolished some time in the 13th century.

Bedlam (Liverpool Street): St Mary Bethlehem Hospital, or Bedlam as it was commonly called, was in medieval times located near what is now Liverpool Street station. It survived the Great Fire, but was nevertheless rebuilt in nearby Moorfields in the 1670s. That building, too, is long gone. The hospital moved once again in 1810 to what is now the Imperial War Museum.

Biscuit Town (Bermondsey): Peek Freans' biscuit factory once dominated the area south of what is now Bermondsey tube. Known affectionately as Biscuit Town, the complex gave the world the chocolate digestive, garibaldi and bourbon biscuit. It closed in 1989.

Bucklersbury House (Mansion House): A sprawling 1950s office complex, demolished in 2010. The ancient course of the River Walbrook was found beneath, along with many important Roman artefacts.

Catch-Me-Who-Can (Euston Square): London's first passenger railway only went round in circles, but Trevithick's engine was ahead of its time. His track was on the site of UCL, and ran three decades before trains came into nearby Euston station.

Christ Church (Lancaster Gate): This landmark church was largely demolished in 1977, thanks to dry rot. The spire still stands, and now forms part of a residential development.

Cripplegate (Barbican): A long-lost gateway into the Square Mile, which gave its name to a wider area around what is today the Museum of London. It was bombed to smithereens in World War II, and is now replaced by part of the Barbican estate.

Diorama (Regent's Park): The Diorama building still stands, but its contents are lost. Like the nearby London Colosseum, it housed impressively huge paintings, which would be cleverly illuminated for a paying audience who sat in a rotating auditorium. It opened in 1823 and closed in 1851.

Dust Hill (King's Cross): King's Cross is, of course, already named after a lost structure – an unpopular monument to George IV, which stood for just 15 years from 1830 to 1845. The area has many other lost features, however, including a smallpox hospital, a suspended railway and this delightful mound of dust.

Earl's Court (Earl's Court): The name of this tube station remains the same on our map to reflect the departure of the Earl's Court exhibition centre, demolished in 2016 to make way for a new housing estate.

Euston Arch (Euston): You can see our artist's impression of this, demolished in the 1960s, on page 81.

Farriner's (Monument): The famous bakery of Thomas Farriner (or Faryner) on Pudding Lane, where the Great Fire of London is believed to have started. Not only was this building consumed, but also 80% of the City of London.

Flower Market (Covent Garden): Covent Garden had served as a market for flowers, fruit and vegetables

---

ABOUT THE MAP

The Lost London Tube Map is from an original idea by Londonist's own Matt Brown; TfL own the copyright to the official tube map, though, so we asked Mark Watkinson to design us a new version. We're a fan of its futuristic wires-and-circuit-board look; maybe in an alternative universe right now someone is using this to navigate an entirely different London Underground.

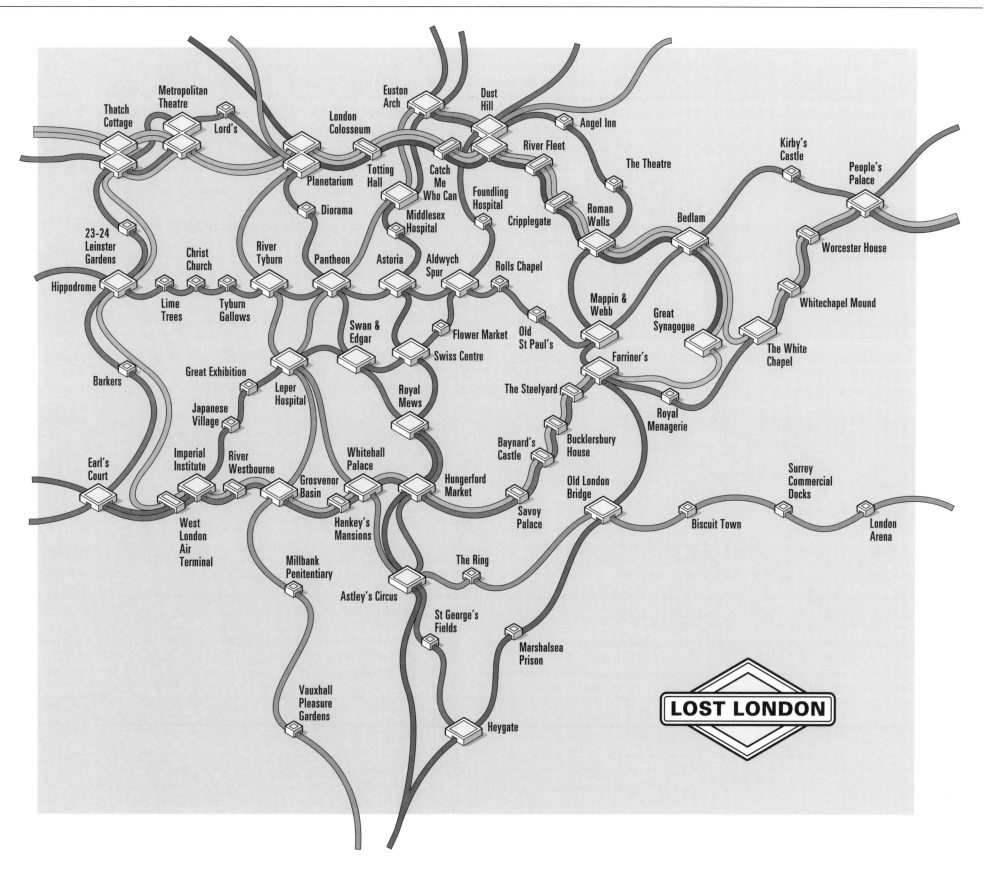

since the 17th century. The logistics of supplying a central London market finally got the better of it, and the produce was carted off to Nine Elms in 1974.

Foundling Hospital (Russell Square): A home for abandoned children was opened by Thomas Coram in the fields north of Holborn in 1739. Most of the buildings were demolished in the early 20th century. The legacy lives on, however, with a children's playground and the nearby Foundling Museum.

Great Exhibition (Hyde Park Corner): The south side of Hyde Park was the original location of the Crystal Palace, built to house a grand exhibition of the wonders of empire. The remarkable glass building was taken down the following year and rebuilt in Sydenham, giving its name to the wider area.

Great Synagogue (Aldgate): After the return of the Jews to England in the 17th century, a great synagogue was constructed in Duke's Place near Aldgate. It went through several rebuilds, but remained in continuous use until it was destroyed by enemy action in 1941.

Grosvenor Basin (Victoria): Victoria station is built on top of a large canal basin, which was appropriated in 1858. Staff still refer to one area of the station as 'the beach', a reference thought to hark back to its watery origins.

Hankey's Mansions (St James's Park): Built between 1873 and 1877, Queen Anne's Mansions was nicknamed Hankey's Mansions after developer Henry Hankey. At 12 storeys high, it was the tallest residential block in the country at that time. Queen Victoria was reportedly miffed as it blocked her view of Westminster from the palace, and its looming presence led to new planning laws limiting tall buildings. It was demolished in 1973 to make way for the even more imposing Home Office building, now the Ministry of Justice.

Heygate (Elephant and Castle): One of London's most recent lost places is the Heygate Estate. The vast housing area at Elephant and Castle accommodated 3,000 people in imposing concrete blocks built in the 1970s. The whole lot has now been demolished, to be replaced by modern housing (much of it prohibitively expensive) in a development known as Elephant Park.

Hippodrome (Notting Hill Gate): The central swathe of Notting Hill was once occupied by a race course. The Hippodrome lasted from 1837 to 1842.

Hungerford Market (Embankment): A produce market, built in the 17th century on the site of Hungerford House at Charing Cross. It survived until the 1860s, when it was swept away by Charing Cross station and the rail bridge which still bears its name.

Imperial Institute (South Kensington): We cover this one in more detail on page 80.

Japanese Village (Knightsbridge): From 1885 to 1887, Londoners flocked to see the Japanese Village at Humphrey's Hall, Knightsbridge. This featured more than 100 actual Japanese people doing actual Japanese things in a not-actual Japanese setting. Imagine.

23–24 Leinster Gardens (Bayswater): Two houses had to be demolished along Leinster Gardens during construction of the what is now the Circle line; the gaping wound in the terrace was patched over with convincing façades, which remain to this day. The peculiar fakery was highlighted in an episode of the BBC's *Sherlock*.

Kirby's Castle (Bethnal Green): A large manor house then asylum in Bethnal Green. It was pulled down in the 1890s; the land is now partly occupied by the library.

Leper Hospital (Green Park): Before St James's Palace, the most notable building in the Piccadilly area was a home for lepers. It was dedicated to St James the Less, hence the name of the later palace and wider area.

Lime trees (Queensway): Kensington Gardens was badly affected by the Great Storm of 1987, losing around 200 trees – many of them mature limes.

London Arena (Canary Wharf): The 15,000-capacity London Arena lasted for just 25 years before being demolished in 2006. Its site is now occupied by the hula-hoopy Baltimore Tower.

London Colosseum (Great Portland Street): The Colosseum was an impressive domed building to the east of Regent's Park. It housed Thomas Hornor's panorama of London, said to be the largest painting in the world. It was demolished in 1874.

Lord's (Marylebone): Thomas Lord's original cricket ground, used by Middlesex Cricket Club, occupied land around Dorset Square from 1787 to 1810.

Mappin & Webb (Bank): This one, at No.1 Poultry, is also on page 80.

Marshalsea Prison (Borough): The setting for much of Dicken's *Little Dorrit*, this debtors' prison near Borough station also detained the novelist's father. It was largely demolished in the 1870s after debt ceased to be a prison-worthy offence.

Metropolitan Theatre (Edgware Road): This large auditorium off Edgware Road had Tudor roots, but was knocked down in 1964 to make way for the Westway.

Middlesex Hospital (Goodge Street): The hospital closed in 2005 and has since been almost entirely demolished to make way for the Fitzroy Place mixed-use development. The ornate chapel and one façade remain.

Millbank Penitentiary (Pimlico): A large prison designed on the principles of Jeremy Bentham, it lasted from 1816 to 1890. Its distinctive outline can still be traced in the layout of local streets, and a perimeter ditch survives. The site is now occupied by Tate Britain and Chelsea College of Art & Design.

Old London Bridge (London Bridge): The Thames has been spanned here since Roman times, with numerous bridges. The most distinctive and longest standing was the medieval structure, which we go into in more detail on page 72.

Old St Paul's (St Paul's): Christopher Wren's famous domed cathedral replaced a larger St Paul's built during the medieval period, which burnt down in the Great Fire of 1666.

Pantheon (Oxford Circus): Oxford Street's Pantheon was an entertainment venue dating back to 1772, with a central dome reminiscent of its Roman namesake. It later served as an opera house and then a bazaar, before its demolition in 1937. The site is now occupied by M&S.

People's Palace (Mile End): Writer Walter Besant was one of the driving forces behind this Mile End entertainment complex, opened in 1887. It attracted one and a half million people in its first year. Sadly, the venue burnt down in the 1930s. The replacement building is now part of Queen Mary University of London.

Planetarium (Baker Street): The building on the side of Madame Tussauds still stands, but stopped showcasing the cosmos in 2006. It's now full of Marvel superheroes.

The Ring (Southwark): A drum-shaped building near modern Southwark station, used as a Methodist church from 1783 to 1881. It thereafter became a famous boxing ring, but was destroyed in two bombing raids in World War II. The site is now taken by the Palestra Building, while a local pub namechecks the Ring.

River Fleet (Farringdon): Not 'lost', as such, but buried beneath the surface and now functioning as a sewer. We've mapped it with Farringdon, but it also flows close to Blackfriars, King's Cross, Camden Town and Kentish Town stations.

River Tyburn (Bond Street): Like the Fleet, the Tyburn is often described as a 'lost river', though in reality it is still gurgling beneath the pavements as a sewer. It once flowed above ground, close to modern day Bond Street station. The route of the watercourse can easily be identified by looking at a street plan of Marylebone and Mayfair. Most streets follow a grid-like pattern, except for those that once tracked the banks of the Tyburn.

River Westbourne (Sloane Square): Yet another 'lost river'. This one can almost be seen at Sloane Square tube, where the waters are carried over the tracks in an iron pipe.

Rolls Chapel (Chancery Lane): This building stood, in various guises, on Chancery Lane from the 13th century right up until the late 19th, when it was demolished to make way for the Maughan Library. It had originally served as a house for converted Jews, but later became a public record office, and a store for charters, patents and other 'rolls'.

Roman walls (Moorgate): The ancient Square Mile was once ringed by fortifications, first laid down by the Romans and subsequently strengthened in medieval times. Most of the wall is now lost, though fragments remain in the Moorgate area as well as near Tower Hill and in various basements.

Royal Menagerie (Tower Hill): From ancient times until the 19th century the Tower of London was home to the royal collection of exotic animals, including elephants, lions and even a polar bear. A series of escapes and mishaps saw the animals decanted over to the new London Zoo in 1832.

Royal Mews (Charing Cross): Today, the site on Trafalgar Square is occupied by the National Gallery. From the 14th century to the 19th it was home to the king or queen's horses and carriages.

Savoy Palace (Temple): A magnificent medieval townhouse on the Thames, owned by John of Gaunt. It was torn apart during the Peasants' Revolt of 1381 and later replaced by the equally grand Savoy Hospital. That too is long gone but its chapel has survived, hidden down a side street. Today, the Savoy Hotel and Theatre occupy the site.

The Steelyard (Cannon Street): From the 15th to the 17th centuries this riverside enclave was populated by the Hanseatic League, a community of German and Dutch merchants. Its activity dwindled after the Great Fire, and the site was eventually cleared by the construction of Cannon Street station.

St George's Fields (Lambeth North): A large open space covering parts of Southwark and Lambeth, roughly centred on St George's Circus. The fields were gradually filled in through the 18th and 19th centuries and the area is now almost entirely built up.

Surrey Commercial Docks (Canada Water): Although Rotherhithe still contains a few remnant docks, notably around Surrey Quays, the network of pools was vastly greater in the 19th and first half of the 20th century. Most of the docks were filled in between the 1970s and 1990s for housing developments.

Swan & Edgar (Piccadilly Circus): A popular department store that inhabited the western side of Piccadilly Circus for over 100 years, closing in 1982.

Swiss Centre (Leicester Square): Not the prettiest of buildings, the Swiss Centre was a treasured cultural venue on the western edge of Leicester Square. It was demolished in 2007 though some of the paraphernalia survives, including the glockenspiel clock.

Thatch Cottage (Paddington): According to *The London Encyclopaedia*, the last remaining thatched cottage in inner London survived in the Paddington area until the 1890s, when it was demolished to make way for St David's Welsh Church.

The Theatre (Old Street): A Shoreditch playhouse on Curtain Road owned by James Burbage. The theatre was dismantled in 1598 and slowly shifted over to Bankside, where it rose again as The Globe (itself destroyed by fire in 1613).

Totting Hall (Warren Street): Also called Tottenham Court, a former manor house where Tottenham Court

Road now meets Euston Road. It was converted into a pub sometime in the 17th century, and was painted by Hogarth. Any remnants were cleared away during construction of the Euston underpass in the 20th century.

Tyburn Gallows (Marble Arch): The notorious execution site – also known as Tyburn Tree – is still famous, more than 230 years on from the last hanging. A discreet plaque marks the supposed spot near Marble Arch.

Vauxhall Pleasure Gardens (Vauxhall): One of London's major entertainment zones between the mid-17th and mid-19th centuries. The gardens hosted many attractions, including music and performance, acrobatics and balloon ascents, and were infamous as a place of nocturnal misadventure and assignation – basically, shagging in the bushes. The gardens closed for good in 1859; the name has been recently reapplied to an open space in the area.

West London Air Terminal (Gloucester Road): During the late 1950s, it was possible to check in to Heathrow Airport via a terminal building near Gloucester Road – miles from the airport.

The White Chapel (Aldgate East): The small chapel of St Mary Matfelon once stood in what is now Altab Ali Park. You can trace its remains on one of the lawns. The whitewashed medieval church was a notable landmark, from whence the wider area of Whitechapel gets its name. Much rebuilt over the centuries, it was destroyed in a bombing raid in World War II.

Whitechapel Mount (Whitechapel): A noted hillock that once loomed over Whitechapel Road, close to the hospital. It is believed to have been part of the fortifications built around London during the English civil wars, though it may have been more ancient. It was levelled in 1808.

Whitehall Palace (Westminster): A favoured home of the royal family for generations until it burnt down in 1698. Only the Banqueting House – outside which Charles I lost his head – remains, and can be visited by the public. Charles II and Henry VIII also breathed their last here.

Worcester House (Stepney Green): A Stepney manor house constructed in 1597 on an earlier Tudor structure. Its remains were recently excavated by Crossrail archaeologists.

IN SEARCH OF ANGLO-SAXON LONDON

Look around any map of London and you'll find the echoes of long-forgotten individuals. Cena, Padda, Fulla… ancient farmers who had no idea their names would live on down the centuries as Kennington, Paddington and Fulham.

Map by
MATT BROWN | LONDONIST

Valley of crocuses

Could the dairyman whose cheese farm (Ces wican) once graced the banks of the Thames have conceived that his humble business would live forever as Chiswick? People of Croydon: whatever happened to the valley of crocuses (Crogdene) after which your town is named? And who knew that the perennial football chant of 'Wember-ley, Wember-ley, Wember-ley' is actually pretty close to the area's original name of Wemba Lea (Wemba's forest clearing).

We've never seen these Anglo-Saxon hamlets and farms mapped out before, so we thought we'd give it a go. The period shown covers 500–1050 AD, between the retreat of the Romans and the coming of the Normans. Once the Romans had cleared off, the area around Londinium was settled by a hotch-potch of Germanic peoples usually termed Anglo-Saxon. Their main trading port of Lundenwic was probably centred on what is now the Covent Garden and Aldwych (meaning 'old port') areas, but we know little about the full extent and organisation of this early London.

Forest, marsh and river

As well as showing the Anglo-Saxon centre, the map also includes many of the villages that surrounded it, with their earliest recorded names. Roman roads, which were still used but probably in ill repair, are also marked, as are tributaries of the Thames.

The extent of woodland at the time is more conjectural. The Anglo-Saxons are known to have felled large portions of forest, and the London area would not have been as woody as you might expect. Still, large expanses of trees, such as the Great North Wood around Sydenham, Epping Forest and the large Middlesex Forest to the northwest were extant. We've also made a stab at showing areas of marsh and flood plain as well as hills around London, although these are imprecise.

Note also that the map covers a period of more than 500 years. Not all the features shown on the map would have been present at the same time. And many additional settlements, and particularly Anglo-Saxon roads, are no doubt missing.

Taking root

It's relatively easy to recognise some of the places we know today in their Anglo-Saxon roots, but others take a little more puzzling out. Vermudesi, for instance – we now know it as Bermondsey. Rederheia might become Rotherhithe, and for Giseldone read Islington. You could be forgiven for not recognising that Gillingas might one day become Ealing, and journalists are probably relieved not to be reporting on the annual Wunnemanndunne Tennis Championships. It means the hill where Winebeald lived.

Many sources were used to piece the map together, but the most useful were *What's in a name?* by Cyril Harris and the *Times History of London* by Hugh Clout, which includes a sizeable gazetteer of name origins.

ABOUT THE MAP

This particular map is the work of the Londonist *team itself, drawn from our own research and added to with the help of our readers – a truly crowdsourced map, you could say. Its full extent can be viewed on the* Londonist *website.*

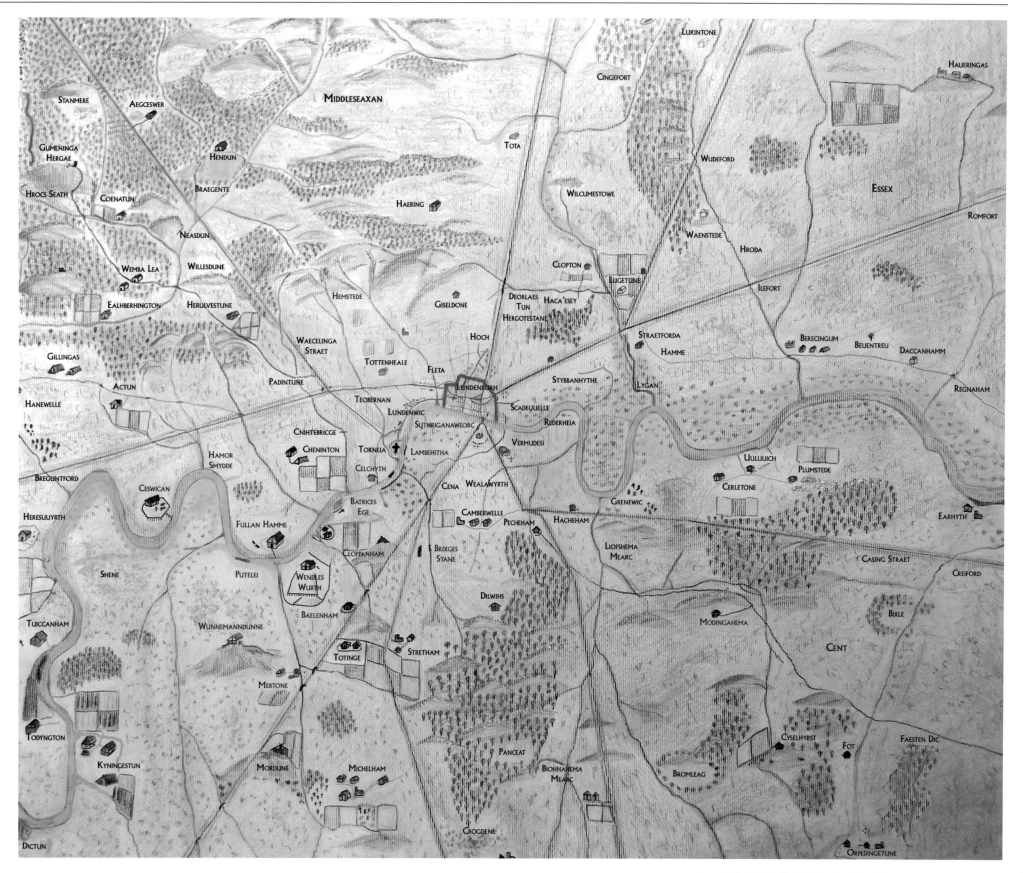

STANMERE
AEGCESWER
GUMENINGA HERGAE
HENDUN
BRAEGENTE
HROCS SEATH
COENATUN
NEASDUN
WEMBA LEA
WILLESDUNE
EALHBERHINGTON
HERULVESTUNE
GILLINGAS
WAECELINGA STRAET
ACTUN
PADINTUNE
HANEWELLE
BREGUNTFORD
HAMOR SMYDDE
CESWICAN
HERESUUYRTH
FULLAN HAMME
TORNEIA
CNIHTEBRICGE
CHENINTON
CELCHYTH
BATRICES EGE
SHENE
PUTELEI
CLOPPANHAM
WENDLES WURTH
BAELENHAM
TUICCANHAM
WUNNEMANNDUNNE
TOTINGE
STRETHAM
TODYNGTON
MERTONE
KYNINGESTUN
MORDUNE
MICHELHAM
DICTUN
CROGDENE

MIDDLESEAXAN
TOTA
HAERING
HEMSTEDE
GISELDONE
TOTTENHEALE
FLETA
TEOBERNAN
LUNDENWIC
SUTHRIGANAWEORC
LAMBEHITHA
CENA WEALAWYRTH
CAMBERWELLE
PECHEHAM
BRIXGES STANE
DILWIHS
PANCEAT
BIOHHAHEMA MEARC

LUKINTONE
CINGEFORT
HAUERINGAS
WUDEFORD
ESSEX
WILCUMESTOWE
ROMFORT
WAENSTEDE
HRODA
CLOPTON
LUGETUNE
ILEFORT
DEORLAES TUN
HACA'ESEY
HERGOTESTANE
STRAETFORDA
HAMME
BERECINGUM
BEUENTREU
DACCANHAMM
HOCH
LUNDENBURH
STYBBANHYTHE
LYGAN
REGNAHAM
SCADEUUELLE
REDERHEIA
VERMUDESI
UULUUICH
PLUMSTEDE
CERLETONE
GRENEWIC
HACHEHAM
EARHYTH
LIOFSHEMA MEARC
CASING STRAET
CREIFORD
MODINGAHEMA
BIXLE
CENT
CYSELHYRST
FOT
FAESTEN DIC
BROMLEAG
ORPEDINGETUNE

ON PIGEONS

The feral pigeon is the single most-spotted bird in London. They flock to the squares, scavenge the streets for food, and defecate on buildings. Their feathered cousin, the wood pigeon, is London's most common garden bird. Some Londoners cherish the city doves, others loathe them.

Map by
REWATI SHAHANI

Trafalgar Square

Tottering around on their little stumps-for-feet, pooing down on us from above, menacingly approaching as we scoff our lunchtime sarnies: Trafalgar Square is certainly popular with London's pigeons – but why?

The Square has been at the heart of Westminster since construction began in the 1830s. According to travel writer Tim Moore's book, *Do Not Pass Go*, pigeons began flocking to Trafalgar Square before building was completed in 1844.

Feed sellers soon established themselves on the square, flogging bags of seed to visitors throughout the Victorian era. These feed sellers could be the key to why Trafalgar Square became so popular with pigeons in particular, rather than with other urban birds.

According to the RSPB, pigeons – descendants of the rock dove, which have been domesticated in the UK for eggs and meat since the Norman invasion – are capable of remembering both faces and places. If fed they will return to the same location and look for the same people, a sort of self-fulfilling pigeon prophecy: the more people that fed them, the more pigeons returned to the square.

Pigeons are also unusually relaxed around groups of people compared to other birds; another reason Trafalgar Square is especially appealing to them.

Rats with wings

The last licensed bird feed vendor on Trafalgar Square was Bernard Rayner, whose family sold seeds in the square for half a century. He was forced off his pitch in 2001 after then-mayor Ken Livingstone decided to ban licensed sellers in the area. Concerned that the birds' acidic poo (lovely) was damaging Nelson's Column and other structures, authorities started installing anti-pigeon wires and spikes.

Feeding the birds in the main square was criminalised in 2003, but animal rights protesters continued to feed pigeons on its North Terrace. Westminster City Council extended the ban to the wider area in 2007, and whacked a potential £500 fine on top. Even more dramatic was the enlisting of Harris hawks to regularly patrol the Square (along with their handlers) and scare the birds away, at a cost of almost £60,000 a year.

Although Livingstone was criticised for the excessive costs of the avian expulsion, a hawk is still present daily. Contrary to previous reports, we found no evidence of feathery carnage. Just a Harris hawk named Lemmy, who likes to perch on the Olympic Clock. He is one of a team of hawks who are regularly flown at Trafalgar Square.

The Greater London Authority isn't the only one employing hawks to deter the pigeons. The Wimbledon tennis championships, condemned by PETA for cruel and illegal culling of pigeons in 2008, apparently has one called Rufus. And the BBC has followed suit with a Harrier hawk for its new headquarters.

Feathered Friends

But there was a time when pigeons were considered heroes. During World War II about 250,000 homing pigeons were employed as military messengers by the Royal Air Force, 32 of whom received a Dickin Medal for their bravery. There's a special display about Pigeons at War at Bletchley Park in Milton Keynes. Lest we forget, they star in the animated film *Valiant*.

London is also home to the famous and widely loved Brian, the world's first blogging pigeon. Although Brian is known to ride on the Piccadilly Line, others have been seen on the District and Central Line.

The biggest fallacy about urban pigeons is that they are a health hazard. They carry diseases like all other animals, but with good hygiene practices the risk of infection is in fact negligible. You're more likely to be struck by lightning. There is no need to worry about bird flu either.

For those who want to feed them, pigeons love sunflower seeds. They just hoover them up. It's best to always check if feeding is allowed at a particular site. And don't forget to wash your hands afterwards.

ABOUT THE MAP

'This work shows London, with large pigeons roughly forming the shape of the city's boroughs and boundaries. Pigeons, at least in the sense of the unattractive and dirty 'London pigeon', are an urban creation; a far cry from the plump, infinitely more charming wood pigeons found outside cities in the countryside. Whether Londoners or visitors hold affection or repulsion for these scrawny, grime-blackened birds, they remain a prevalent feature of London's urban landscape – and character.'
- Rewati Shahani

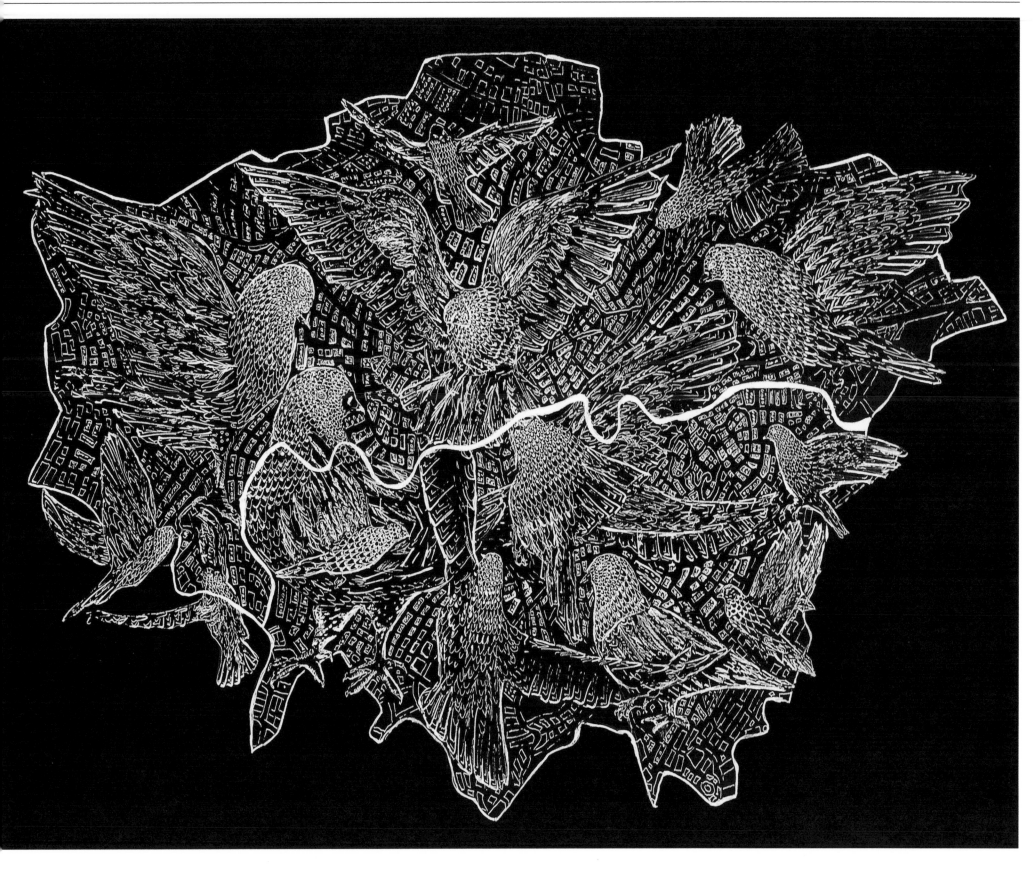

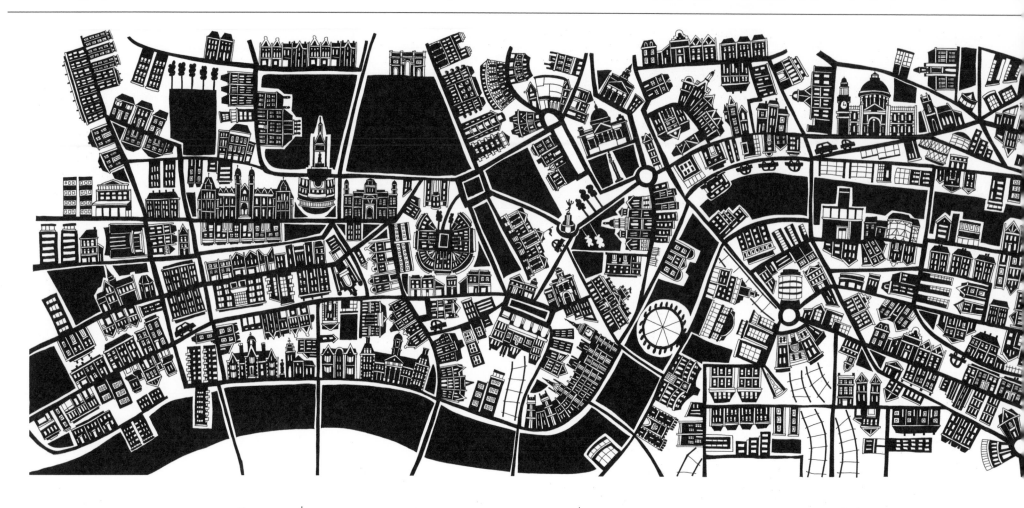

SECRETS OF THE THAMES

It's one of the key focal points of the city and the reason London sprung up in the first place – the River Thames is what many of us think about when we think of the capital. But how many of these facts did you know about it?

The beginning

The source of the Thames is in a spring in a field in Gloucestershire, but for London the river starts at Teddington. It is here, at Teddington Lock, that the river ceases to be tidal. The Thames was tidal all the way to Staines until 1811, when the controversial new barrier was built. It threatened the livelihoods of locals who fished and worked the river, and was so unpopular that the lock-keeper was armed with a blunderbuss and a brace of pistols. After the old London Bridge was demolished in 1831 the river level dropped, and Teddington Lock had to be rebuilt to stop barges running aground.

The end

The Thames is still officially river not sea until it reaches an invisible line in the estuary, between Westcliff-on-Sea in Essex and the Isle of Grain in Kent. The boundary, the edge of the Port of London Authority's patch, is marked with a stone on either bank.

On the Kent coast a small obelisk sits in the middle of nowhere, in the mud of Yantlet Creek, and is known as the London Stone. The Essex version is called the Crowstone, and is rather more accessible on the beach at Westcliff, handy for the promenade.

Purfleet forest

Purfleet, best known for its oil refinery and as the place where Count Dracula stepped ashore, is surrounded by the open expanses of the Essex marshes. But here on the flatlands is a hidden forest, only visible at low tide.

To the west of Purfleet, the mud has preserved a tangle of tree trunks more than 6,000 years old. Ash, elm and alder from a long-lost forest were preserved in layer of brown peat beneath the river mud. The trees belong to the Neolithic era, and flint tools found here hint at the hunter gatherers who roamed the Thames shore.

Pickle Herring

The riverfront space where City Hall sits, surrounded by accountancy firms in glass boxes, used to be the heart of London's docks. Nowadays Docklands means the Isle of Dogs and City Airport, but until the 1960s some of the most intense activity was on Tooley Street. The river from London Bridge to Tower Bridge was a wall of wharves,

Map by
LUCIE CONOLEY
ILLUSTRATION

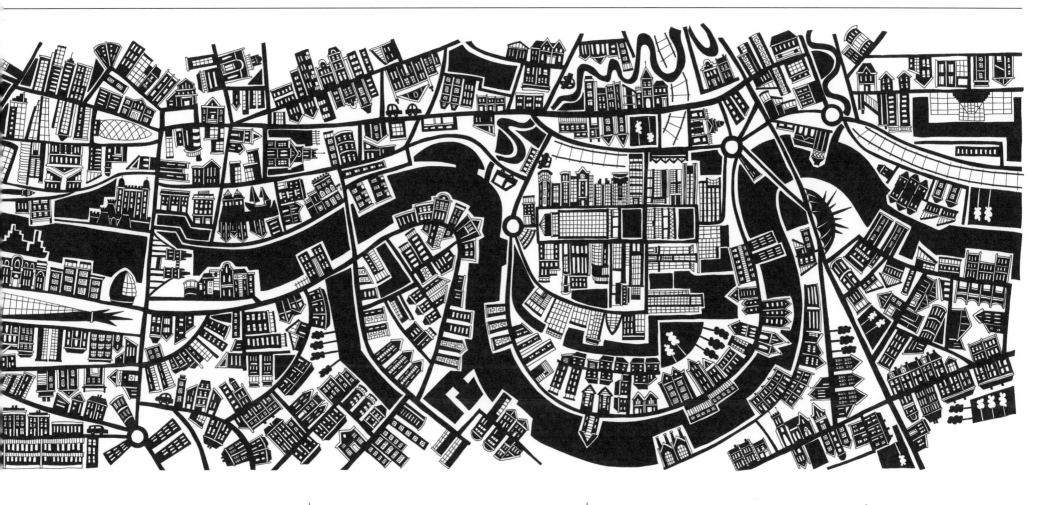

many handling perishable goods from Europe such as German cheese and Polish bacon. This was London's Larder, and at its heart was Pickle Herring, an ancient, narrow street probably named after its top import. Pickle Herring was a continuation of Shad Thames and looked just like it, narrow and criss-crossed with iron bridges. It was demolished in the 1970s, an act of destruction hard to imagine now.

Sailor Town

Redclif, Ratcliff, Ratcliffe: it's not just the spelling of London's first port that is hard to pin down. Before the great, enclosed docks of the 19th century were hollowed out of Limehouse, Rotherhithe and the Isle of Dogs, ships docked at Thameside wharves. The most sheltered place on the river was in the crook of the bend at Limehouse, at a place called Ratcliffe or Sailor Town. Ratcliffe was one of the original Tower Hamlets, named after a lost cliff of red earth, shovelled away as ballast for the great ships that left its quays. These were London's earliest docks, where Tudor expeditions led by adventurers like Sir Hugh Willoughby set sail for the Arctic. The 19th century saw

Ratcliffe eclipsed by its neighbours, and although it is marked on maps few know of its existence.

London's lighthouse

The River Lea meets the Thames at Bow Creek, where it goes through an extravagant set of meanders. This gives us the oddly shaped Leamouth Peninsula, home to Trinity Buoy Wharf and its pocket lighthouse. Not exactly located on rocky coastline, it was in fact a training lighthouse built in the 1860s to test lighting designs and coach lighthouse keepers. It closed in 1988 and the peninsula became arts space, and the site of a big Crossrail hole. The lighthouse now houses ex-Pogue Jem Finer's astonishing *Longplayer*, a piece of music that plays automatically and lasts 1,000 years. It's due to finish at midnight on 31 December, 2999.

A time bomb

Peer out to sea from the port of Sheerness-on-Sea, at the mouth of the Thames Estuary, and you will see what look like three masts protruding from the waves. This is the wreck of the *SS Richard Montgomery*, a US cargo ship.

In August 1944, a couple of months after D-Day, she crossed the Atlantic from Philadelphia loaded with more than 6000lb of munitions, including a stock of super-large Blockbuster bombs. The ship dragged its anchor, ran aground and broke up on the Sheerness sands. More than 70 years later, no-one really knows how dangerous it is, but they do agree that it could explode spontaneously. At the very least, the blast would send up a tidal wave and break every window in Sheerness.

The Tilbury graffiti wall

Alongside the Thames between Grays and Tilbury, half a mile of concrete flood wall has been sprayed with ambitious designs on a large scale. The wall is invisible from the shore unless you climb down to walk by the water, but it hides murals from Asterix to the Silver Surfer to Roy Lichtenstein. It goes back a long way, at least to the days when people stencilled Mod slogans.

The wall is only accessible on foot, preferably while trekking the Thames from source to sea, but the strange and beautiful art is well worth the journey.

ABOUT THE MAP

Sometimes a map can be both complicated and simple at the same time, and this one completely fits the bill. The original, if you're interested, is 22ft long and 5ft tall, and can be found at One Canada Square.

HOW TO EAT, DRINK AND SMOKE LIKE WINSTON CHURCHILL

Despite his penchant for food, liquor and cigars, Winston Churchill reached the ripe old age of 90. While we wouldn't suggest consuming the goodies listed here in one go, we reckon dabbling in the odd one or two should be fine.

Map by
LOUISA JONES ILLUSTRATION

Eat

One non-boozy liquid that Winston adored was soup. He'd eat a bowl of cold consommé before bed, even if he'd just returned from a slap-up dinner at The Savoy. Thin, non-creamy soups were what Churchill hankered after – and that applied to his turtle soup too. This he once served up to President Roosevelt, after a Commander Thompson spotted a couple of tins in a Piccadilly grocers and took the rare commodity back to Number 10.

The corpulent PM would regularly round off dinner with a cheese platter. And there was one London fromagerie he regarded above all others: 'A gentleman only buys his cheese at Paxton & Whitfield,' Churchill once said. Fortunately for the gentlemen (and women) of today's London, Paxton & Whitfield is still in business. We have it on good authority that his cheese of choice was a Swiss gruyère.

Churchill also adored his Indian curries (so there are plenty of places to commemorate him all across the capital). However, he wasn't keen on Chinese (sorry, Chinatown), or sauerkraut (apologies Herman ze German).

Drink

History is giddy with anecdotes of Churchill's drinking. You may think a man who started the day with a whisky or brandy must have been a raging lush – but Churchill's morning tipple was heavily diluted (you should still only attempt this if you're off work for the day), and many historians say he was rarely actually blotto.

That's not to say he didn't get through gallons of booze. According to historian Sir David Cannadine, Conservative politician and Chancellor of the Exchequer Rab Butler had no fewer than eight huge meals foisted on him at Downing Street during 1955, all washed down with libations of brandy. So much brandy that Butler was forced to pour some of it down the sides of his shoes. Whether the dinner guest had to squelch his way out of Number 10 is not recorded.

Champagne was Churchill's greatest weakness, or strength, as he liked to put it. 'In success you deserve it and in defeat, you need it,' he quipped. The champagne on Churchill's rider was a very specific one – Pol Roger – and Churchill tended to buy it from Berry Brothers & Rudd on St James's Street, where you can still pick up a bottle today (the cheapest costs under £40).

Smoke

Winston fell in love with Havana cigars when he was a journalist in Cuba. Back in London, he eagerly put in his first order for imported Cubans at Robert Lewis on St James's Street. Nowadays, that shop is James J Fox – and that very same order can still be seen written in a big ledger.

It's reckoned that Churchill smoked in the region of 200,000 cigars in his lifetime. Although, to be fair, he likely chewed his way through half of them. In fact, Churchill would usually slobber through just half a Cuban before chucking it.

On the town

Hosting dinner parties was a forte of Churchill's that ranked alongside his diplomatic skills. But he liked to dine, drink and smoke out, too. It was at The Savoy that Churchill, along with Lord Birkenhead, formed The Other Club – a political dining society where Winston would glug expensive brandy, shoot the breeze with his compatriots, and – according to Cita Stelzer in *Dinner With Churchill: Policy-Making at the Dinner Table* – re-enact battles with salt-and-pepper shakers for hours at a time.

Stelzer's book also includes some fascinating insight into how Churchill had no qualms about questioning his bills. A 1934 correspondence between Churchill's private secretary and The Savoy begins with a letter that claims:

'Mr Churchill is surprised at the amount of this bill, which works out at almost £3 a head.'

The overcharging is subsequently blamed on a bottle of port that was only half drunk, to which The Savoy replies that the remainder is '…being kept at the bar for Mr Churchill's use next time we are honoured with his patronage.'

Among other Churchill haunts you can get to is Browns Hotel on Albemarle Street, which was frequented by the PM so often it's rumoured they built a bomb shelter for him in there (although we couldn't confirm this). The bar here does a Churchill Martini (essentially a glass of gin).

One last thing

Along with dodging bar bills, it transpires Churchill once swerved a £197 invoice at Savile Row tailors Henry Poole & Co because he didn't much fancy paying it. Henry Poole is still there today, if you feel like dressing like the great man. We strongly recommend paying all invoices.

ABOUT THE MAP

For centuries, this is where the London gentleman of means shopped: tailored shirts from Savile Row; shoes from Jermyn Street perhaps; champagne and cigars from St James's Street, before retiring to his gentlemen's club (also, of course, in the area). We asked Louisa Jones to map a few of the best-known and longest-standing locations – and a spiffing job she's done of it too.

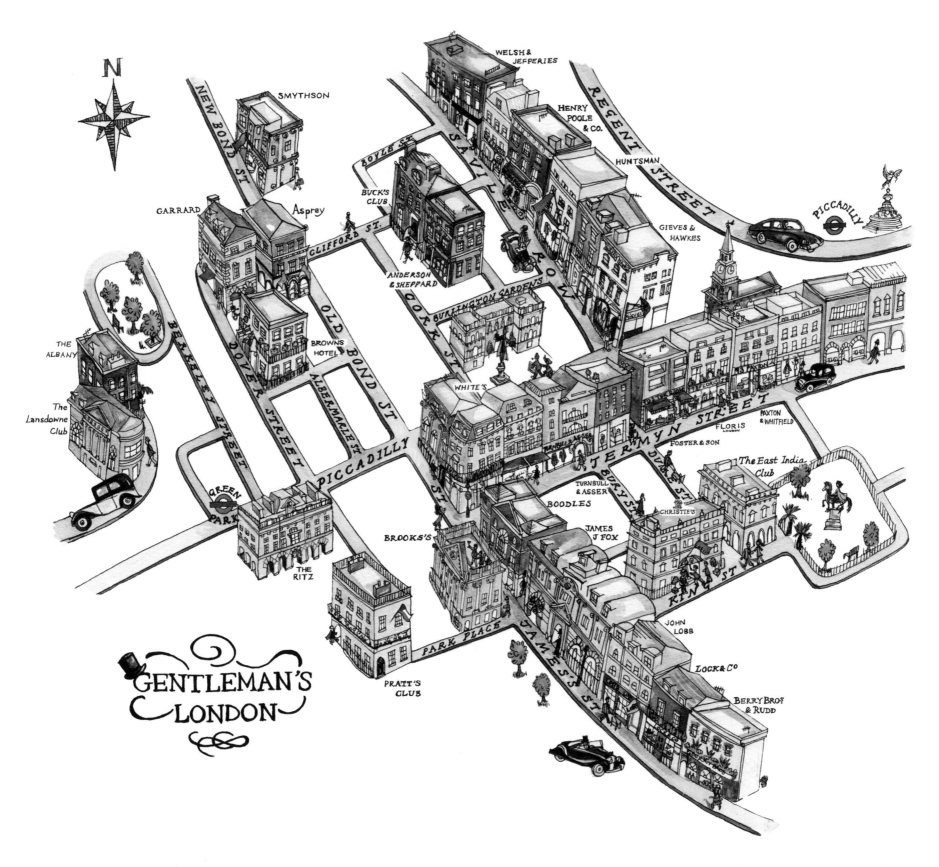

N

SMYTHSON

WELSH & JEFFERIES

REGENT STREET

HENRY POOLE & CO.

HUNTSMAN

PICCADILLY

NEW BOND ST

BOYLE ST.

SAVILE ROW

GARRARD

Asprey

BUCK'S CLUB

GIEVES & HAWKES

CLIFFORD ST.

ANDERSON & SHEPPARD

CORK ST.

OLD BOND ST.

BURLINGTON GARDENS

THE ALBANY

BROWNS HOTEL

WHITE'S

BERKELEY STREET

DOVER STREET

ALBEMARLE ST.

The Lansdowne Club

FLORIS

JERMYN STREET

PAXTON & WHITFIELD

FOSTER & SON

The East India Club

TURNBULL & ASSER

GREEN PARK

PICCADILLY

BOODLES

DUKE ST.

BURY ST.

CHRISTIE'S

JAMES J FOX

BROOKS'S

THE RITZ

PARK PLACE

JAMES'S ST.

KING ST.

JOHN LOBB

LOCK & Co

PRATT'S CLUB

BERRY BROS & RUDD

GENTLEMAN'S LONDON

TOP 10 LONDON SOCIAL BENEFACTORS

In a city of increasing divide between its richest and poorest, it feels timely to take a look at those philanthopists who invested in our city for social good. Listing them in chronological order it's notable that the majority are 19th-century philanthropists. The only one still alive (at the time of writing) is rather surprising.

Map by
AMY BRIDGES

Captain Thomas Coram (1668–1751)

The Foundling Museum and neighbouring park at the eastern extremes of Bloomsbury were once part of the Foundling Hospital, a refuge and school for abandoned infants. This worthy institution was set up by Thomas Coram in 1739, becoming the world's first incorporated charity.

George Peabody (1795–1869)

George Peabody made his money in the USA and came to London in 1827 where he lived and worked for many years. On seeing the poverty and slums, he resolved to help the working poor. The first Peabody estate was built in Spitalfields, then came estates in Islington, Shadwell, Westminster and Chelsea. Each estate had a play area for children, while the shared toilets were monitored for diseases. The Peabody Group now owns and manages around 20,000 homes across the capital.

Anthony Ashley-Cooper, 7th Earl of Shaftesbury (1801–1885)

Politician and social reformer, Lord Shaftesbury was president of the Ragged Schools Union for nearly 40 years. Set up to provide free education to destitute inner city children, it is estimated that during the good Lord's tenure 300,000 London children were taught trades. He also campaigned for better conditions in asylums, for the rights of child chimney sweeps, a reduction in the working hours of mill workers, and animal rights. Shaftesbury lent his name to the Shaftesbury Park Estate in Battersea, 1,200 houses with gardens built specifically for the working classes, as well as Shaftesbury Avenue and the Shaftesbury Memorial.

Angela Burdett-Coutts (1814–1906)

Scion of the loaded Coutts banking family, Angela found herself the wealthiest woman in England upon her inheritance of 1837. She poured great sums into helping the working classes, funding numerous churches, societies, schools, housing schemes and even drinking fountains for dogs.

John Passmore Edwards (1823–1911)

A self-made man, as well as a great Victorian reformer, Passmore Edwards believed that by 'funding the ladder, the poor may be encouraged to climb.' He built hospitals, drinking fountains, libraries, schools, convalescent homes, art galleries and the Passmore Edwards Settlement in Tavistock Place. Among his many benefactions are the Canning Town Boys Club, East Ham Hospital, Tilbury Cottage Hospital, a children's holiday home in Clacton, Whitechapel Gallery and South London Art Gallery.

Andrew Carnegie (1835–1919)

A lowly Scot who at the age of 12 was working in an American cotton factory, Andrew studied hard and invested wisely, eventually becoming the richest man in the world. When he sold his steel company in 1901, Carnegie trousered $225 million and embarked on a suitably grandiose plan to educate the world, building 3,000 libraries (380 in Britain). London has Carnegie libraries in Brentford, Crofton Park, Hanwell, Herne Hill, King's College, Leyton, Sydenham, Teddington and Twickenham. Bromley knocked theirs down.

Octavia Hill (1838–1912)

Although she donated less personal wealth than others on this list, Octavia Hill's contributions to society through dogged campaigning were so immense that she surely deserves a place here. With financial help from John Ruskin, Hill set up many experiments in social housing throughout the capital (one example can be seen today at Red Cross in Southwark). She also campaigned to save open spaces, such as Hampstead Heath, for recreation, and was one of the founders of the National Trust.

Thomas John Barnardo (1845–1905)

Still a household name thanks to his extant charitable organisation, Barnardo made a major contribution to alleviating Victorian poverty by establishing homes for children. The first of 112 opened in Stepney in 1870. By the end of his life, an estimated 100,000 children had benefited from his efforts. A museum devoted to Barnado's works can be found at the Ragged School.

Sir Henry Wellcome (1853–1936)

Sir Henry established a fortune from the pharmaceutical industry. He also amassed a magnificent collection of cultural artefacts relating to medicine and health. After his death, Sir Henry's moneybags were poured into the Wellcome Trust. This is now the largest charity in the UK, funding medical research. The Trust also funds a wing of the Science Museum, and acts as a major partner in the Francis Crick Institute research centre behind the British Library. Sir Henry's collection of cultural artefacts forms the core of the Wellcome Collection on Euston Road.

Richard Desmond (b. 1951)

Yes, the one time publisher of *Asian Babes, Horny Housewives, Readers' Wives* and *40 Plus* has a giving nature. As the drummer with the RD Crusaders, whose members have included Roger Daltrey, Robert Plant and Lulu, Desmond has raised around £14 million for charitable causes and also finances the Richard Desmond Children's Eye Centre at Moorfields Eye Hospital.

ABOUT THE MAP

Artist Amy Bridges's intricate map of the area south of the Thames is packed with details about the area and the people who lived there. We spotted Octavia Hill, but Emma Cons and Lilian Baylis are two more women who left their mark on this area – grab a magnifying glass and take a look.

HOW LONDON'S THAMES BRIDGES GOT THEIR NAMES

Believe it or not, there are 35 bridges* over the Thames in London.

*Pedants' note: depending how you count. The Golden Jubilee Footbridges and Hungerford Bridge all cross at the same point, and might be considered as one bridge or three, depending on the context. In addition, the Teddington crossing comprises two separate spans linked to an island.

Map by
LIS WATKINS ILLUSTRATION

The furthest west, Hampton Court Bridge, is only just within the Greater London boundary. The furthest east, Tower Bridge, is pretty much in the centre of London. (The Dartford Crossing, known as the Queen Elizabeth II Bridge, is outside the London boundary.) Here we look at the origin of their names.

Hampton Court Bridge (1933)

This is now the only bridge in London that crosses over into another county (Surrey). Its red-brick span with classical stylings were designed (partly by Sir Edward Lutyens) to match nearby Hampton Court Palace, after which it is named. The Palace in turn takes its name from the nearby village of Hampton, originally an Anglo-Saxon settlement whose name probably derives from a small farmstead on a bend in the river (Hamm + ton).

Kingston Bridge (1828) and Railway Bridge (1863)

Kingston-upon-Thames, on the ancient Wessex/Mercia border, was a stupendously important place in medieval times. As many as eight English kings might have been crowned here, and the putative coronation stone on show near the Kingston Guildhall is one of London's oldest monuments. No surprise, then, that the name simply means 'King's estate'. It was first recorded in 838 as Cyninges tun.

Teddington Lock Footbridges (1887/89)

Teddington is the point where the river ceases to be subject to the tides. For this reason, some have claimed that the name is a corruption of 'tide's end town'. This is not so, for the tidal reach would have been further upstream in ancient times. It's thought that Teddington is derived from a personal name, perhaps a local landowner, and was first recorded as Totyngton in the Anglo-Saxon period. You can cross at this point via a combo of suspension and girder bridges.

ABOUT THE MAP

Squeezing all 35 of London's Thames bridges onto one map is no easy feat, but Lis Watkins has somehow managed it for us – we love how she's managed to pick out the individual details of each bridge. Thanks to Sadiq Khan, though, for sparing us from having to fit in a 36th.

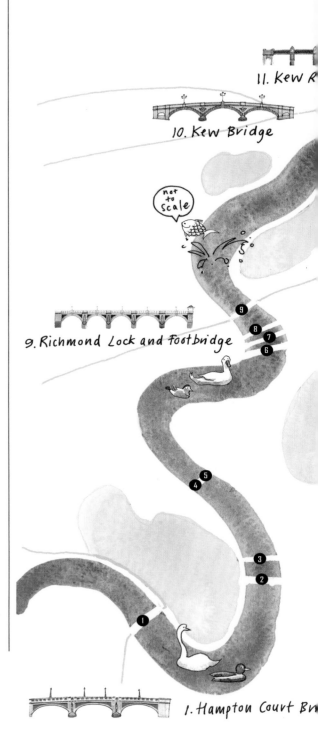

11. Kew R

10. Kew Bridge

not to scale

9. Richmond Lock and Footbridge

1. Hampton Court Br

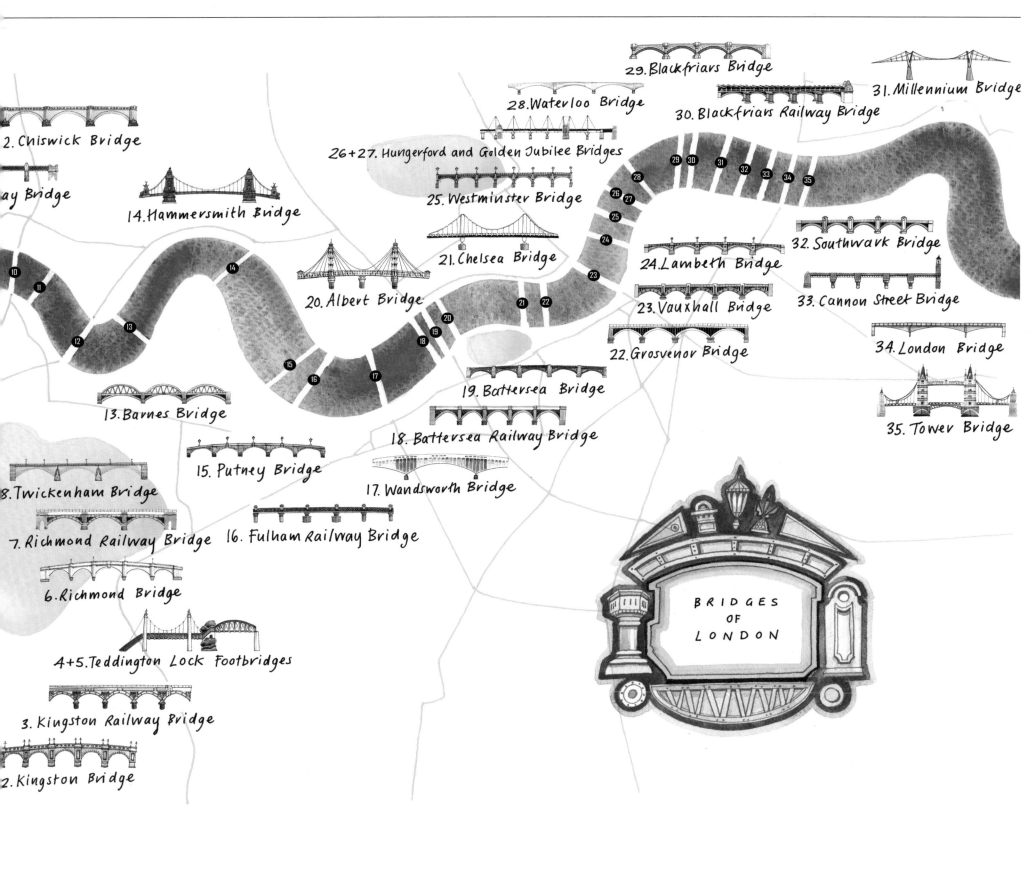

29. Blackfriars Bridge

31. Millennium Bridge

28. Waterloo Bridge

30. Blackfriars Railway Bridge

2. Chiswick Bridge

26+27. Hungerford and Golden Jubilee Bridges

...ay Bridge

25. Westminster Bridge

32. Southwark Bridge

14. Hammersmith Bridge

21. Chelsea Bridge

24. Lambeth Bridge

33. Cannon Street Bridge

20. Albert Bridge

23. Vauxhall Bridge

34. London Bridge

13. Barnes Bridge

22. Grosvenor Bridge

19. Battersea Bridge

35. Tower Bridge

18. Battersea Railway Bridge

15. Putney Bridge

17. Wandsworth Bridge

8. Twickenham Bridge

7. Richmond Railway Bridge   16. Fulham Railway Bridge

6. Richmond Bridge

BRIDGES OF LONDON

4+5. Teddington Lock Footbridges

3. Kingston Railway Bridge

2. Kingston Bridge

Richmond Bridge (1777), Railway Bridge (1848) and Lock Footbridge (1894)

The only surviving London Thames bridge from the 18th century, Richmond Bridge and its two neighbours are, of course, named after the adjoining settlement. But that place is not as ancient as some might think. Before Tudor times, the area was known as Sheen (still in use, further from the river). Around 1500, Henry VII built a Thames-side palace here, naming it after his North Yorkshire Earldom of Richmond. That northern territory was, in turn, named after Richemont in Normandy, which translates rather predictably as 'rich hill'.

Twickenham Bridge (1933)

Twickenham might be intimately associated with rugby, but the namesake bridge has closer associations to football – it was designed by the same architect (Maxwell Ayrton) as the old Wembley Stadium. The name has been around since at least 704AD, when a document refers to the land as Tuiccanham. The original meaning is uncertain. It may refer to the land of a man called Twicca, or else derive from the word twicce, which meant river fork (this being near the place where the rivers Thames and Crane meet).

Kew Bridge (1903) and Railway Bridge (1869)

Odd name, Kew. It's thought to be a contraction of Kai, meaning landing place (hence 'quay'), and Hoh, meaning a spur of land. Another interpretation has the name meaning a key-shaped piece of land. Either way, it's first recorded in 1327 as Cayho.

Chiswick Bridge (1933)

In one of our favourite derivations, Chiswick is Old English for 'cheese farm', and was first recorded as Ceswican around the year 1000.

Barnes Railway Bridge (1849)

The combined rail-footbridge takes its name from the nearby settlement of Barnes, which is first recorded in the Domesday Book as Berne, probably referring to a barley store (i.e. a barn).

Hammersmith Bridge (1887)

Hammersmith has disputed origins as a place name. Some sources suggest it derives from Hammoder's Hythe (a safe haven belonging to Hammoder), others, perhaps more satisfyingly, suggest it's simply a concatenation of 'hammer' and 'smithy', denoting an area important for metal working.

Putney Bridge (1886)

Like Hammersmith, the origins of Putney are murky. It's first recorded in the Domesday Book as Putelei, but where that term comes from, nobody is sure. Some sources make a link to the Old English word Putta, meaning hawk, though it could equally stem from a personal name.

Fulham Railway Bridge (1889)

Fulham was an area belonging to an Anglo-Saxon called Fulla, but rather than the usual 'ham' meaning homestead, this one was originally 'hamm', signifying a bend in the river.

Wandsworth Bridge (1939)

Bridge, town and borough all take their names from the River Wandle, which remains one of the delights of the area. The Wandle got its name from an Anglo-Saxon called Waendel, who owned land round here.

Battersea Bridge (1890) and Railway Bridge (1863)

Another Anglo-Saxon name, Battersea was originally recorded as Badrices īeg, meaning the island of Badric. In ancient times the Thames would have been much wider and shallower, creating small islands where there is now continuous land. St Mary's Battersea was the centrepiece of one such island where the Falconbrook met the Thames.

Albert Bridge (1873)

Like a precursor to the Millennium Bridge, this delicate pink-and-green structure was known as the 'trembling lady' after its opening, thanks to its tendency to vibrate when large numbers of people walked in sync. Signs at either end still request that troops break step when marching across. It's named, of course, after Albert, consort to Queen Victoria – partly in tribute to the late prince, but also because its construction had been his idea.

Chelsea Bridge (1937)

Chelsea crops up in various ancient spellings along the lines of Chelchith, meaning the landing place or wharf for chalk. Chalk was a useful commodity used in fertiliser. This raises the interesting notion that the phrase 'as different as chalk and cheese' might have its origins among the medieval denizens of Chelsea and Chiswick.

Grosvenor Railway Bridge (1859)

This is the railway bridge heading out of Victoria station and across to Battersea – and also London's widest bridge, although it might also be considered as 10 parallel spans rather than one bridge. It was the first railway line to cross over the Thames and was originally called Victoria Bridge (as, occasionally and confusingly, was nearby Chelsea Bridge). It gets its name from the Grosvenor family, upon whose land Victoria station was built (and before that, the Grosvenor canal and basin). The Grosvenor name can be traced back to Hugh Le Grande Veneur, one of the French nobles who came across with William the Conqueror. The name translates as 'the master huntsman', making this the only London bridge to be named after a blood sport.

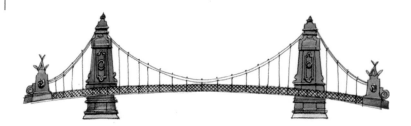

Vauxhall Bridge (1906)

Another Anglo-Norman soldier puts his name to this bridge. Falkes de Breauté was a 13th-century knight who built a hall in this part of south London. It became known as Falkes' Hall and eventually Vauxhall. His legacy continues in several other guises; the Vauxhall car company uses Falkes' griffin device for its own logo.

Lambeth Bridge (1932)

Rather satisfyingly, the name means 'landing place for lambs', and it's a shortened version of the earlier Lambehitha (hitha being a common ending for riverside landing places like Rotherhithe).

Westminster Bridge (1862)

The name relates to the famous Abbey – 'mynster' being Old English for a church. The 'West' part simply denotes it as west of the ancient City, and its great church of St Paul. In Anglo-Saxon and early Norman times, the area was known as Torneia or Thorney Island, for an islet of that character, upon which the abbey and Palace of Westminster are built.

Hungerford Bridge and Golden Jubilee Footbridges (1864/2002)

Hungerford's one of those names that's all but vanished from the map, but it was once a well known market where Charing Cross station now stands (a small echo of market stalls can still sometimes be found hidden away at the raised level between the station concourse and the pedestrian bridges). The market got its name from Hungerford House, which occupied the site until its destruction by fire in 1669. The Golden Jubilee Footbridges were appended in the 21st century to celebrate Queen Elizabeth II's 50th year in the same job (imagine the redundancy package she must be entitled to by now).

Waterloo Bridge (1817/1945)

The bridge was under construction at the time of the famous battle (1815), in which the forces of Napoleon were defeated by Wellington and von Blücher. It was to have been called Strand Bridge, but the military victory immediately prompted calls for a 'Bridge of Waterloo'. The span opened two years later as the slightly snappier Waterloo Bridge. Problems with the foundations led to the original bridge being demolished in the 1930s and a replacement, designed by Sir Giles Gilbert Scott, was constructed during World War II by a largely female workforce. The Belgian place name Waterloo translates roughly as 'wet clearing in the forest'.

Blackfriars Bridge (1869) and Railway Bridge (1886)

The two bridges are named for a priory of the Dominican order, established at the foot of Ludgate Hill in 1276. Dominican friars traditionally wore black garments, and hence their hangout became known as Black Freres (black brothers) and later Blackfriars. These are therefore the only bridges to get their names from an article of clothing.

Millennium Footbridge (2000)

Also known as the Wobbly Bridge, thanks to a now-corrected eccentricity, the pedestrian span has a rather obvious official name, opening around the turn of the Third Millennium. Although this is one of the capital's newest bridges, plans had been kicking around since at least the 1920s to build a crossing at this point.

Southwark Bridge (1921)

This ancient part of London was settled by the Romans. Early records call it Suthriganaweorc or Suthringa geweorche, meaning 'the defensive works of the men of the south' (i.e. Surrey).

Cannon Street Railway Bridge (1866/1982)

Counter-intuitively, this bridge and the street that it serves have nothing to do with either religious canons or explosive cannons. Cannon Street is, rather, a 17th-century shortening of Candelwrichstrete – the street of candle makers, as first noted in 1190. The origins are still hinted at today; Cannon Street falls within the Ward of Candlewick, one of 25 ancient subdivisions of the City of London.

London Bridge (1973)

Some form of bridge has existed on or near this site since Roman times, and for many centuries it was the only fixed crossing in the capital. Only natural, then, that it should take the name of the city it serves.

Tower Bridge (1894)

No mystery here. Tower Bridge is right next to the Tower of London. This medieval palace gets its own name from the White Tower, the keep at the heart of the complex, which was once coated in whitewash.

BUILDINGS THAT SURVIVED THE GREAT FIRE OF LONDON

The Great Fire of London in 1666 consumed about four-fifths of the City. Some buildings escaped, but most have since been demolished or destroyed in the Blitz.

Map by WENCESLAUS HOLLAR, 1666–67
Printed in WILLIAM MAITLAND'S HISTORY OF
LONDON, 1756

Yet, here and there, one can still find traces of the pre-fire city. Here we look at the survivors within the Square Mile or just beyond.

Around Smithfield

London's ancient livestock market largely escaped the blaze. Look out for the Golden Boy of Pye Corner, who marks the extent of the conflagration on Giltspur Street. The streets north of this boundary contain one of the richest collections of pre-fire buildings.

41/42 Cloth Fair: The oldest house in the Square Mile, this multi-storey dwelling was completed in 1614. After a long period in the doldrums, it is once again in use as a private residence.

St Bartholomew-the-Great: One of London's most atmospheric churches, St Bart's looks like no other building in central London. That's because it's very old. Parts of the church, like the Romanesque arches, date back to Norman times. Look out, too, for the Tudor gatehouse which faces onto Smithfield.

Charterhouse: A former priory, then school, parts of which date back to the 16th century, Charterhouse has long contained almshouses for the elderly.

Guildhall

Few sites in the City are so entangled in history as the Guildhall. The complex contains architecture from many periods, from the remains of a Roman amphitheatre to the late 20th-century art gallery. Although damaged by the Great Fire and the Blitz, plenty of medieval stone can still be seen. The grand front is a Georgian pastiche, but the main hall and crypt are proper old.

City churches

Churches were the most prominent buildings of the pre-fire city. Eighty-seven churches succumbed to the flames, along with St Paul's Cathedral. Not all perished, though.

St Olave Hart Street: The parish church of fire chronicler Samuel Pepys avoided a fiery fate by a whisker. The flames halted just a block to the west. Much of the building dates from 1450, though it's heavily restored after damage in the Blitz.

St Helen's Bishopsgate: Shakespeare's parish church also had a lucky escape in the Great Fire. The flames stopped just a little to the southwest. The church also got through the Blitz largely unscathed. Sadly, two IRA bombs in 1992 and 1993 caused extensive damage.

St Andrew Undershaft: Another church in the shadow of the Gherkin, St Andrew also survived both the Great Fire and the Blitz. It dates from 1532.

St Katharine Cree: Nearby, this Tudor church also fell outside the fire zone. The tower dates from 1504, while the nave is from 1630(ish).

St Giles-Without-Cripplegate: Outside the city walls, St Giles was spared the ravages of the fire. Alas, it took a right old hammering in World War II.

All Hallows by the Tower: The church was saved after surrounding buildings were demolished as a firebreak. All Hallows was gutted in the Blitz, but stonework from 1658 remains (a rare church building from the Commonwealth era). Inside is an even older survivor – a Saxon arch from an earlier incarnation of the church.

St Etheldreda's: The famous enclave of Ely Place off Holborn contains one of the City's oldest buildings – St Etheldreda's dates back to at least 1290. It is also one of the oldest Roman Catholic churches in England.

City pubs

Ye Olde Cheshire Cheese on Fleet Street (see page 84) might feel like one of the City's most venerable pubs, but its present form dates from just after the fire. At least three other venues can claim a longer pedigree.

Hoop and Grapes: This Aldgate mainstay was built in 1593, a welcome bit of humanity in an area now dominated by glass tower blocks.

Olde Wine Shades: Although it's just 100m from the source of the Great Fire, this wine bar somehow survived the disaster. The building dates from 1662.

Seven Stars: Just outside the Square Mile, the Seven Stars deserves a place in this list for its character and charm. The tiny boozer is thought to date back to 1602.

The Temple

The historic legal enclaves of Inner Temple and Middle Temple contain many old buildings. The most noted is the drum-shaped **Temple Church**, which found worldwide fame thanks to *The Da Vinci Code*. The church goes back to the late 12th century, but was heavily rejigged by Christopher Wren. Still more impressive is **Middle Temple Hall**, which harks back to 1573. The building was already several decades old when it hosted the first performance of *Twelfth Night* in 1602.

ABOUT THE MAP

This engraving of the City of London was printed in 1756, but is based on an original map of 1666–67, immediately after the Great Fire. The blank areas of the map represent the ruins left by the fire, with few buildings left standing.

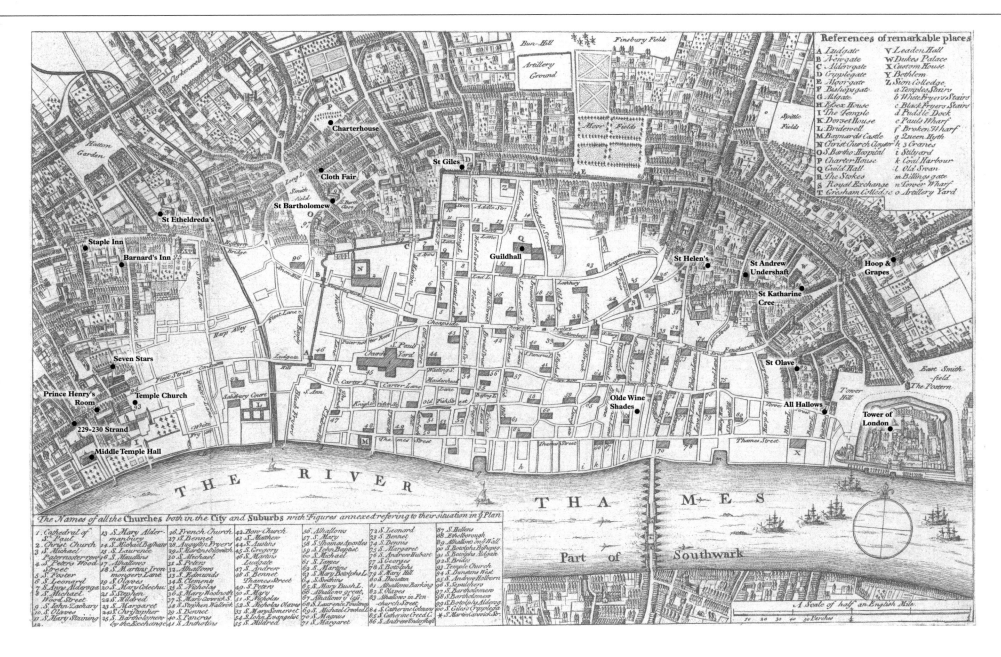

Along Fleet Street

Prince Henry's Room: Number 17 Fleet Street has been much altered over the centuries, but still retains much of the timber frame from 1610. The Great Fire was stopped just a few doors east of here.

229–230 Strand: 'The only Strand building to survive the Great Fire of London', claims a plaque above the door. It's not true. Every building on the Strand survived the Great Fire – the flames never troubled this road.

The Hall at Lincoln's Inn is still older (1490), but a little further from the fire boundary (and off-map).

Staple Inn and Barnard's Inn

One of London's more famous Tudor buildings, **Staple Inn** squats next door to Chancery Lane tube station. The timber-framed confection is ostensibly from 1585, but is heavily restored. The row was a good distance from the western-most reach of the fire.

Nearby **Barnard's Inn** is also well known thanks to its use as a venue for the popular Gresham College lectures. Much of the hall dates from the 15th century. The roof is said to contain the only crown post in Greater London.

It should probably read 'to survive the Great Fire and everything since'.

Tower of London

It goes without saying that London's oldest substantial building – begun in the 1080s – is a Great Fire survivor.

The Tower is not technically in the City of London, but is such an important building that we include it for completeness.

The flames, in fact, came very close to the fortress. The Tower's guard saved their own skins by blowing up nearby buildings, creating a firebreak. It's just as well they did. The Tower contained an estimated 500 tonnes of gunpowder. Had it gone up, tourists would today be visiting the Vast Crater of London.

STATELY HOMES OF SOUTHWEST LONDON

Most of London's grander inner-city houses-with-parks are long gone (give or take the odd palace), but head upriver and it's another story.

Map by
DEBBIE RYDER

Chiswick House

Chiswick House is a beautiful neo-Palladian building in a stunning garden setting. It is also, however, a slightly dubious starter on a list of great homes and houses, as it was never intended as such. The building was created in 1729 as a bold architectural experiment by the Earl of Burlington, who sought somewhere impressive to show off his artwork.

You can still find plenty of fine art at Chiswick, but the gardens are the real star, with a series of spectacular features and vistas.

Kew Palace

Located in Kew Gardens, the current palace is the second of three; little is known of the first, while the third stood for less than 30 years in the early 19th century. The second one, originally known as the Dutch House, dates back to 1631 and has been under royal ownership since the 18th century. Come for the incredible gardens, stay for the palace.

Syon House

Syon House is one of the few stately properties in the region still used as a residence. The Duke of Northumberland calls it home, as his ancestors have done for 400 years. It's pretty much your textbook stately home, with a succession of Robert Adam interiors and sweeping Thames-side gardens. Consequently, it pops up in more films than Owen Wilson – including the most recent *Alice Through the Looking Glass*. Look out for the rooftop lion, which once stood on another Northumberland property at Charing Cross.

Osterley House

No one posh has lived here for the best part of a century, but this one-time seat of the Child family (bankers) still sparkles with class. From the outside, the 18th-century house is relatively bland; dull even. The inside, however, is a different story.

At Osterley Park and House, Robert Adam (yes, him again) created some of the most ostentatious rooms in the capital. If you're a fan of interior design it might make your eyes bleed. There's also a Tudor stable block once owned by Royal Exchange founder Sir Thomas Gresham (but precious little information about it). Check out the gardens, too.

Marble Hill House

Marble Hill House was originally built for King George II's mistress, Henrietta Howard. A portrait of her hangs in the house, part of a collection of early Georgian paintings.

Ham House

Few buildings have a better aspect than Ham House, which nestles on that particularly pleasant stretch of Thames between Richmond and Twickenham. There's plenty to see inside this early 17th-century building, now administered by the National Trust. You'll find a fairly typical, if not dazzling, cavalcade of period furniture, paintings and grand gestures. The gardens are well kept and a pleasure to stroll around.

Strawberry Hill

No other building in the country quite compares with Horace Walpole's mock-Gothic pile of Strawberry Hill, located near Twickenham. The 18th-century house was recently restored with a £9 million grant. It's like a stately home and a cathedral somehow managed to produce offspring, with arched doorways, screens and stained glass round every corner. Tours are popular, and you're encouraged to prebook before your visit.

Hampton Court Palace

This was originally built by Cardinal Wolsey (1473-1530), the Archbishop of York and chief minister during the early part of Henry VIII's reign. When he fell from favour after failing to get Henry's marriage to Catherine of Aragon annulled, Henry took the place for himself. It's been a royal palace ever since, although George II was the last monarch to live there.

ABOUT THE MAP

It took us a moment to work out what was unusual about Debbie Ryder's map of southwest London – have you spotted it yet? It is, of course, its orientation; it's upside down. South is now north; east is now west, and we're very confused. The artist explains: 'I like to use a bird's eye view for my maps and felt this 'reverse' use of the River Thames suited my way of working, was an aesthetically pleasing composition and also provided the best solution to include all the landmarks I wanted to illustrate.'

A GUIDE TO TUBE PEDANTRY

We all love a bit of pedantry. At the same time, is there anything more annoying than a quietly cleared throat, followed by an 'I think you'll find…'? Plenty, actually. Besides, as a pedant would no doubt remind you, it's all in the details. Here's our guide to tube (or should that be Tube?) pedantry.

Is there a difference between 'the tube' and 'the Underground'?

Yes, and no. Today, the terms are used interchangeably by most people. But that wasn't always the case.

The older lines, such as the Circle, District and Metropolitan, run through large tunnels, with relatively roomy trains. These lines were constructed by 'cut and cover' – in other words, a huge trench was gouged out of the earth, and then covered over. They're just below the surface and are often covered by roads, such as Euston Road or Embankment. From the opening of the first line in 1863, the system was generally known as the London Underground Railway, or the Underground for short.

By contrast, the rest of the network runs through narrower, deep-level tunnels, which were bored rather than scooped. The first, what we now call the Northern line between Stockwell and Borough, opened in 1890. These tunnels were quickly dubbed 'tube railways' because of their circular profile.

For the first few decades of the 20th century, a clear distinction was made between the two types of tunnel. Newspapers talk of the 'underground and tube railways', as though they were separate systems – which they were, with different lines operated by different companies. The system finally came together (mostly) as a unified whole in 1933, with the formation of London Transport.

After this merger, and the publication of the first modern tube maps, passengers began to think of the underground tunnels as part of one, coherent network. The difference between 'tube' lines and 'underground' lines has since blurred, and only the most pedantic, point-scoring person will maintain the distinction. TfL itself concedes that the tube is 'an acceptable colloquial shorthand for the London Underground'.

Should I write 'tube' with a capital letter?

Transport for London tends to capitalise the word 'Tube' in all instances. Some publications, such as *The Times*, follow suit, and this is also preferred in the BBC style guide. Many other publications (including *Londonist* and the *Guardian*) use lower case. A third way is to use upper case when talking about the Tube (as in, the whole network), while using lower case for its more generic attributes, like 'a tube line' or 'a tube station'.

King's Cross or Kings Cross? Earl's Court or Earls Court?

Apostrophes hold an endless fascination for the pedant. They're used with some inconsistency across the transport network, but suffice it to say that both King's Cross and Earl's Court do carry apostrophes (at least on the tube map – Earls Court usually drops its punctuation elsewhere), while Queens Road (Peckham) and Barons Court do not.

Are the Overground routes classified as tube lines?

The London Overground network – the confusing tangle of orange on the tube map – launched in 2007 and has grown several times since. It lumps together numerous existing railways into one network, including the former East London line, which was once a bona fide part of the London Underground (see next section).

Despite appearing on the tube map, and containing former parts of the Underground, the Overground is not classed as part of the tube network. It uses different rolling stock and livery (note the orange roundel versus the tube's red roundel), and is currently operated by LOROL under franchise (whereas the tube is operated by London Underground Ltd, a subsidiary of TfL).

So if it's not part of the tube, why is the Overground on the tube map? What is both colloquially and officially known as the tube map (or Tube map) contains much more than tube lines. It's a way of visualising the services owned by TfL, and also includes the Docklands Light Railway, Emirates Airline (cable car) and the tram system. It does not show services such as Thameslink and the Northern City line as these are not owned or operated by TfL.

It would be wrong to say the tube map shows all TfL services, however. The true pedant could point out that buses and cycle hire, for example, are not reflected on the map.

As a final pedantic note, not all Overground stations are overground, and not all are in London. Likewise, London Underground is mostly overground, and extends beyond the bounds of the capital in several places.

Can I still refer to the East London line?

For decades, the East London line ran from New Cross to Shoreditch. It closed in 2007, got stretched up to Dalston, then reopened in 2010. Many people still refer to the route as the East London line. TfL does not. Not officially anyhow. According to its editorial style guide, 'East London line' is now 'Overground Dalston/Highbury & Islington – West Croydon/Crystal Palace/New Cross'. Which is, of course, utterly ludicrous, quite possibly the longest name for a railway in the world, and surely the only line to have more forward slashes than a typical internet address. Even TfL rarely uses the official name in public communications. Tannoy announcements refer, for example, to 'the Overground to New Cross Gate', rather than the laborious technical name.

ABOUT THE MAP

Francisco Dans has come up with a take on the tube map that makes up for in abstract beauty what it lacks in practicality. His curvilicious design takes Frank Pick's rectilinear, geographical classic and spirals it out from the most densely connected station (King's Cross St Pancras) to the furthest-flung parts of the map (at least that's what we think he's done). Just don't try using it to get to Heathrow; you may unexpectedly find yourself in northeast London.

Map by
FRANCISCO DANS

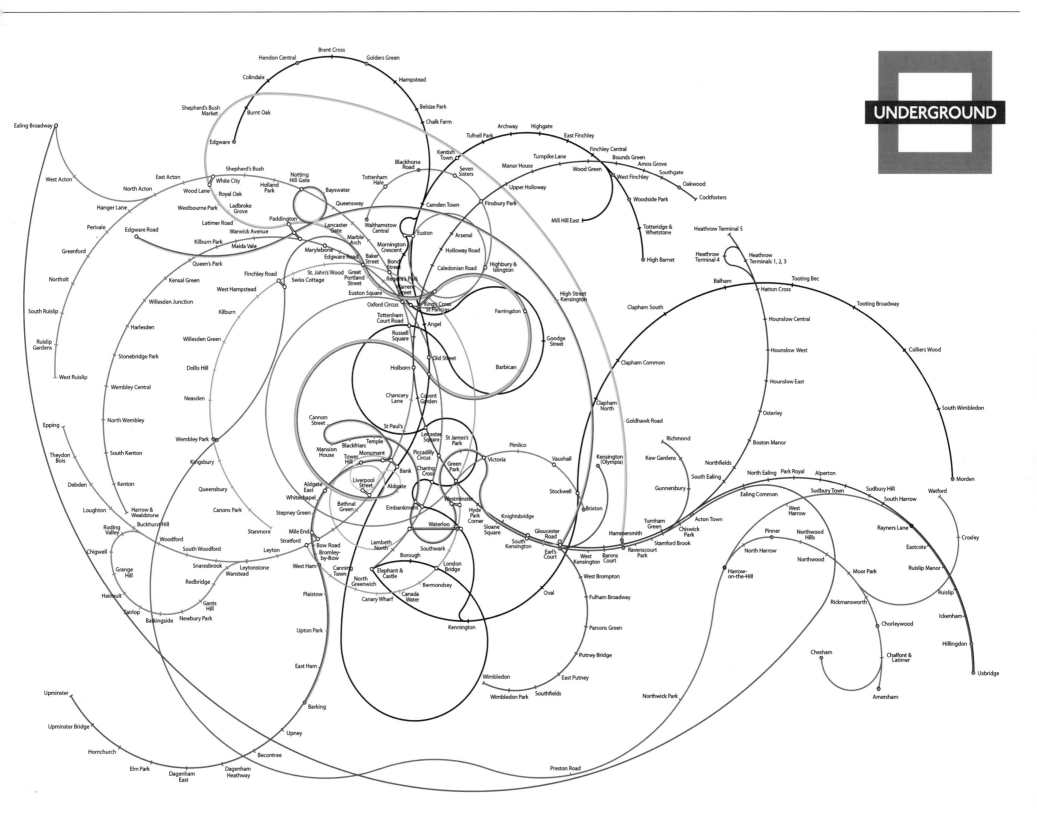

SECRETS OF LONDON'S 'MAGNIFICENT SEVEN' CEMETERIES

London's Magnificent Seven is a collection of grand Victorian cemeteries, scattered around the city. With tombs the size of small houses, they can feel like their own (ghost) towns. Along the way they've picked up their own stories and secrets; we've delved into just a few of them here.

Map by
FREYA HARRISON

Abney Park Cemetery

Abney Park Cemetery: home to London's dissenters, a lion tamer and an Amy Winehouse video…

The lion tamer's grave At first glance, you might think a lion had been buried in Abney Park. Actually, the big white cat marks the grave of Frank Bostock. Known for educating Victorian Britain about African and Asian wildlife, Frank had been a lion trainer since he was 15. He survived both a tiger and lion mauling and had his finger bitten off by an ape. He died of the flu.

A resting place for rebels When the cemetery opened in 1840, it was a burial site for nonconformists, those who rejected the ways of the Church of England, and didn't align with a particular Christian sect. Abney Park is now Europe's longest standing non-denominational chapel. Architect William Hosking was very deliberate in his design, ensuring the chapel in no way showed any bias towards a single Christian sect.

Entertainment is dead Abney Park must be the most entertaining cemetery in the world. Scores of Victorian comedians, pantomime actors and other performers are buried here. These include Albert Chevalier (full incredible name Albert Onésime Britannicus Gwathveoyd Louis Chevalier), songstress and male impersonator Nelly Power, and famous comedian and 'Dame of Drury Lane' panto star Herbert Campbell.

Home to a 170-year-old bush Abney Park Cemetery is home to many rare species of plants and creatures. The oldest recorded tree is a 170 year-old Perry's Weeping Holly, which is actually a bush. Hundreds of species of insects thrive in the cemetery grounds.

Fire, fire, fire You don't really think of cemeteries catching fire, but Abney Park's had its fair share. One fire damaged two common ash trees in the 1890s. On Sir Isaac Watts Walk, a silver birch was struck by lightning, but survived with a long black gash down its trunk. The centre chapel also burned down in the 1970s.

Don't go mushrooming It's not advisable to go mushrooming in Abney Park. Edible plants are likely to be infused with arsenic, from the bodies embalmed in the Victorian era. Mushrooms are also likely to be full of lead because of the lead-lined coffins used by Victorians.

Brompton Cemetery

Brompton Cemetery sits within one of London's most affluent boroughs and is the final resting place of several notable people. Emmeline Pankhurst, one of the leaders of the women's suffrage movement, is buried here.

It's got a time machine… apparently Speculation suggests that the tomb of wealthy socialite Hannah Courtoy is a fully functioning Victorian time machine. Rumoured to be a teleportation device that connects seven different cemeteries, this grand, inaccessible stone tomb – a listed monument – nods to the Victorian fascination with time travel and Egyptian culture. The interior is said to feature ornate hieroglyphics.

One of its residents invented sunglasses… Sir William Crookes was one of the most famed scientists of his era. Unusually for a man of science, Crookes believed in psychic phenomena and held seances in his own home much to the ridicule of his peers. Nonetheless his numerous scientific accomplishments speak for themselves and include the invention of the radiometer, the spinthariscope and a precursor to modern television. Most notably, Crookes's work with ophthalmology led to his development of sunglasses in the early 20th century.

…and the inventor of traffic lights is here too John Peake Knight designed the first traffic lights in the world. They were situated opposite the Houses of Parliament, at the junction of Great George Street and Bridge Street in Westminster, and were gas powered. The lights were consistently manned, but a leaky gas main resulted in one of the traffic lights exploding in the face of a policeman. This shaky start meant it was 40 years before traffic lights would reappear.

Bees thrive in the cemetery Brompton Cemetery has its own apiary, and delicious honey is available during cemetery open days.

An architect's dream Brompton Cemetery is one of the earliest examples of a landscape architect and a traditional architect working together. Designed by

ABOUT THE MAP

We think this map speaks for itself, really; it's Freya Harrison's gallant effort to combine our vast amount of Magnificent Seven trivia into one glorious map. We think it makes hanging out in cemeteries look rather fun, actually.

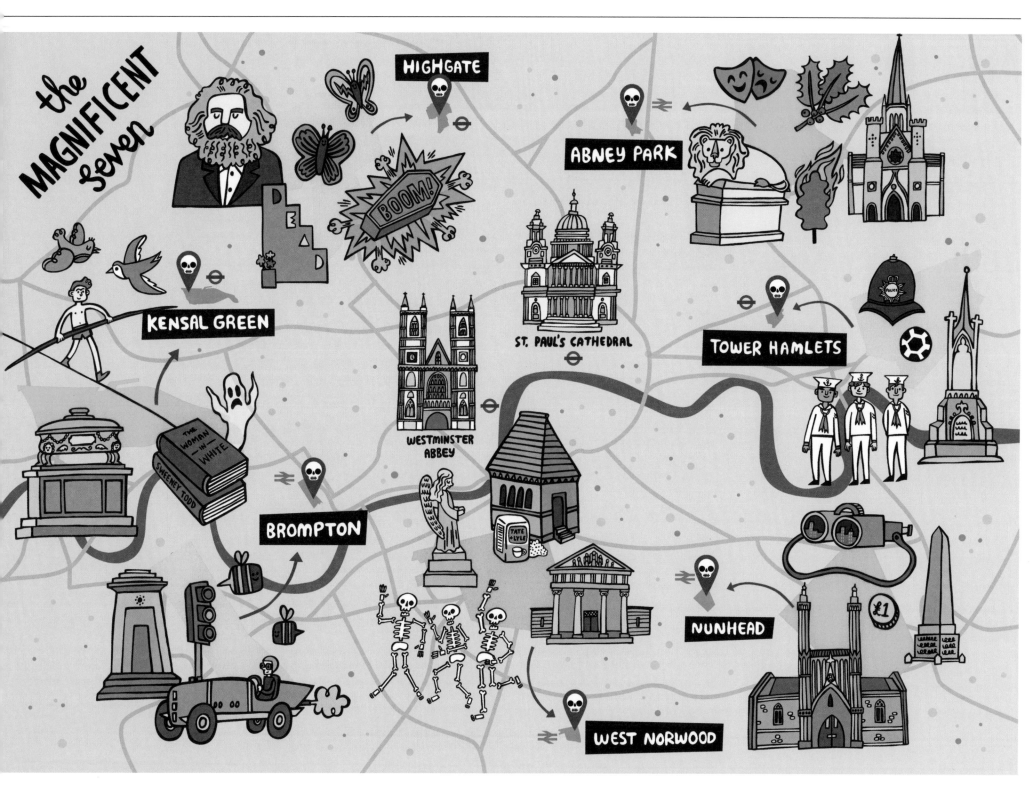

Benjamin Baud and John Claudius Loudon, inspiration for the cemetery was taken from St Peter's in Rome. Baud had won a public competition in 1838 to design the cemetery; unfortunately, his extravagant ideas led the cemetery into financial difficulties and when serious faults appeared in the catacombs he was dismissed.

Ghostly driver Resident racing driver Percy Lambert – the first person to drive at 100mph – was killed in a car crash when his tyre burst at Brooklands race track in November 1913. Visitors to the circuit have often identified the shadow of a silent workman in overalls pointing along the track. It can't be a coincidence that Lambert's gravestone takes on the form of a tyre.

Highgate Cemetery

Highgate Cemetery is perhaps the most famous of the 'Magnificent Seven' burial grounds. It fell into ruin during the early 20th century but is now a popular tourist destination – visitors come to see the final resting place of Karl Marx, George Eliot, Michael Faraday, Douglas Adams and many more.

Britain's great forgotten adventurer The name might not ring a bell but it really should. James Holman is possibly the greatest and bravest adventurer in history. For he did it all blind – his aim to prove that his handicap was a motivator, not a hindrance. One of his greatest achievements was hiking up Vesuvius, then skirting around its rim, claiming that because he couldn't see the drop beneath him, he had nothing to fear. Holman also trekked 3,500 miles to reach Irkutsk in Eastern Siberia. Unfortunately, once he reached his destination, he was sent home – accused of being a British spy.

Leaning to the left The hatred Communism inspired in the 20th century led to many attempts to vandalise and destroy the bust of Karl Marx in the cemetery. One particularly notable attempt came with an attempt to blow it up. This failed miserably, but rather aptly left the statue leaning ever so slightly to the left.

More things are alive here than dead Highgate Cemetery fell into disrepair in the 20th century. While humans had all-but forgotten about the cemetery, the natural kingdom had taken over. Highgate is now home to wildlife including 40 species of birds and 20 different types of butterflies, as well as foxes, owls and badgers.

It's got a radioactive-proof grave Highgate houses many murder victims from the Victorian period. But it's also the final resting place of the victim of one of the most high profile murders of recent times. Alexander Litvinenko was murdered via radioactive poisoning in London's Millennium Hotel in 2006. His body is buried 12ft deep in a lead-lined coffin, to avoid the risk of any visitors contracting radioactive poisoning themselves.

Its most well-attended funeral was the funeral of Thomas Sayers in 1865, which attracted roughly 10,000 people. Sayers was an extremely successful bare knuckle boxer and his career culminated in a fight with American John Camel Heenan, which is widely considered the first (unofficial) world championship bout. The match ended in a draw after nearly two hours, when Heenan attempted to strangle Sayers and the crowd invaded the ring. Sayers died of tuberculosis just four years later. The funeral procession was trailed by the chief mourner, Sayers' dog Lion. He too is memorialised in stone at the gravesite, loyally guarding his master.

The exploding coffins issue The Victorians were obsessed with ancient Egypt, and this translated to their burials: Highgate's catacombs were built for those who wanted to be buried above ground in the Egyptian fashion. This was something of a disaster; regulations stated that those interred in this way had to have their tombs encased in lead, for fear of miasma (gases which Victorians believed caused illness) leaking out. As the bodies decayed, a build-up of noxious gases filled the coffins, and in extreme cases they would explode. Eventually a solution was agreed upon: a small hole would be drilled in the coffin, and a pipe placed in it. A lighted match applied to the pipe resulted in a flame burning off the gases 'hygienically', for up to three weeks.

Postmodern brilliance Highgate Cemetery is still functioning and people are still buried here today. Artist Patrick Caulfield's tombstone is particularly worth hunting down for its rather brutal honesty. Sculpted into it is the word DEAD (and you really can't disagree with that assessment of the situation).

Kensal Green Cemetery

Kensal Green is the city's oldest commercial cemetery. Its designer, George Frederick Carden, based it on Père Lachaise in Paris. It's home to many famous Brits, from Isambard Kingdom Brunel to Harold Pinter.

A tightrope master Charles Blondin, the famous Victorian tightrope walker, is buried in Kensal Green Cemetery. Blondin walked across Niagara Falls in 1859 and decided it wasn't challenging enough, so did the crossing over 300 more times with various hindrances (blindfolds, carrying passengers, pushing a wheelbarrow, and even stopping halfway to cook up an omelette).

It's a conservation area Kensal Green Cemetery was made a conservation area in 1984 and is home to some rare flora and fauna, along with almost a hundred species of bird – so don't forget your trusty binoculars.

Royal trendsetting One of the most popular monuments in the cemetery is that dedicated to Princess Sophia. Sophia lived a rather tragic life, sheltered from the outside world by her father King George III, especially after she bore an illegitimate child she wasn't allowed to keep. Her isolation from the family is what led to her being buried in a public cemetery. This unknown royal perversely gave the newly opened cemetery a mainstream appeal, especially among the aristocracy.

Killed by a coffin This is what happened to an unfortunate soul named Henry Taylor in 1872. Taylor was a pallbearer for a funeral at the cemetery; as he was carrying the coffin he caught his foot on a stone and stumbled. His fellow pallbearers let go of the coffin, which fell on and killed him. Despite it being his place of death, there are no records of Henry Taylor actually being buried in Kensal Green Cemetery.

Missing parts It's no secret that famed scientist and inventor of the first computer, Charles Babbage, is buried at Kensal Green Cemetery. What is less widely known is that not all of him is resting in the ground there; he's lying there without his brilliant brain. Half of the organ is preserved at the Hunterian Museum in the Royal College of Surgeons, whilst the other half is on display at the Science Museum.

Horror pedigree Some of Britain's finest writers chose Kensal Green as their final resting place. Less commonly discussed is the cemetery's association with another genre of the arts; horror. James Malcolm Rymer, the co-creator of everyone's favourite demon barber, *Sweeney Todd*, and Wilkie Collins, author of *The Woman in White*, rest here. The cemetery was also used as a set location for horror films *Theatre of Blood* and *Afraid of the Dark*.

Nunhead Cemetery

Nunhead is the second largest of the Magnificent Seven cemeteries, and probably the wildest. Almost 270,000 people are buried here, dating back as far as 1840.

It only cost £1 Okay, the cemetery cost a lot more to build, but the London Cemetery Company, which had originally owned it, went bankrupt in 1960. In 1975, Southwark Council bought the site for £1. Much of the cemetery is still wild as a result of being left untended for years, with many paths and gravestones inaccessible.

An arson attack The ruined Anglican chapel in the centre of the cemetery was destroyed by arson in 1976. The interior and roof were completely destroyed by the fire, and the catacombs apparently raided for lead and jewellery. The chapel was stabilised in 2001 and, though a ruin, is now used for music and theatre performances. The catacombs were restored at the same time.

The view of St Paul's On the western side of the cemetery, a viewpoint is marked on the map. Climb the hill and you'll be rewarded with the vista of St Paul's Cathedral. The trees are trimmed so as to protect the view.

Bodies from Bank An unknown number of the bodies laid to rest in Nunhead Cemetery were previously buried in the City of London. They came from the churchyard of St Christopher le Stocks, which stood on the site now occupied by the Bank of England's Garden Court.

The Scottish Martyrs Memorial One of the more interesting listed memorials is The Scottish Martyrs Memorial. The obelisk structure doesn't mark a grave, but memorialises five political radicals: Thomas Muir, Fyshe Palmer, William Skriving, Joseph Gerrald and

Maurice Margarot. There is not thought to be any particular connection between the martyrs and Nunhead.

Walworth Scouts Perhaps one of the most shocking memorials in the cemetery commemorates nine young boys aged between 11 and 14. Eight of them were from the 2nd Walworth Scouts who were on a camping and sailing trip on the Isle of Sheppey in 1912 when their boat overturned and they drowned. The ninth was Frank Masters, from the training ship *Arethusa*, who died trying to help them.

Tower Hamlets Cemetery

Tower Hamlets isn't crawling with celebrity and extravagance like Highgate or Kensal Green; the cemetery instead functioned as a burial ground for London's working classes.

Not just for locals A high proportion of those laid to rest here were sailors who drowned at sea, and were buried in Tower Hamlets because the Docklands were so local. Twenty-nine people were buried here in 1871, when the wooden pleasure steamer *Princess Alice* collided with an iron collier called *Bywell Castle*. Most of the victims lie in unmarked public graves.

Blitz debris The Luftwaffe heavily targeted the nearby Docklands during the Blitz, and the cemetery suffered collateral damage. In 1952 a memorial was erected to those who died in the air raids, made out of bricks taken from bombed properties.

Three policemen in one grave Frugality is in the nature of this cemetery, as most of its inhabitants didn't have enough money to pay for elaborate burials or even their own personal plot. A curious example can be found in one grave which holds three policemen. All the men worked at Leman Street Police Station in Limehouse. They did not, as you might expect, die together. The men didn't even die within a close period of time of each other, nor did they all die in the line of service, so there is little explanation for the grave sharing.

The West Ham connection One of the cemetery's most noticeable memorials is Joseph Westwood's 30ft-high towering spire. Westwood ran Joseph Westwood and Co,

a shipbuilding firm. The company evolved into Thames Iron Works, and some of the employees put together a work football team. Thames Ironworks FC later became West Ham United FC. The club still has the nicknames 'The Irons' and 'The Hammers'.

West Norwood Cemetery

West Norwood Cemetery is home to gothic catacombs, Victorian millionaires, and a rather strange railway…

Resting place of a sugar entrepreneur Many notable figures are buried in this grand cemetery, which opened in 1836. Baron Julias de Reuter, founder of the Reuters news agency, has a pink granite obelisk here. Sir Henry Tate, sugar merchant and founder of the Tate Gallery, lies in a pinkish brick mausoleum, as does Royal Doulton bigwig Sir Henry Doulton.

The design of the cemetery is very specific
The world's first-ever Gothic-style cemetery, West Norwood is built on a hill; one of the reasons for this is that it was believed that the raised ground would help prevent spread of disease. Additionally, the chapel, (which was demolished in the 1960s) was positioned so that the whole town could see it – a reminder of man's mortality. And of course, by being on a hill, the dead were that little bit closer to heaven.

Dancing on the dead Enon Chapel, just off the Strand, is best known for its 'Dancing on the Dead' events that went on there in the 19th century. Baptist minister W Howse offered his burial services at a cheaper rate, carrying out up to nine or 10 every Sunday. Beneath Enon Chapel was a cellar – in which Howse stuffed 12,000 corpses. In 1848, Mr George Walker, a surgeon, bought the chapel and had the bodies moved to West Norwood, where they were reburied in a single grave. Not a good afterlife.

The cemetery has a railway track… sort of In 2010, in an exploration of the remains of the Dissenters' Catacombs, a rusty bier (a frame used to move corpses or coffins before burial or cremation) was found. The wheels of the bier had been designed to run on a narrow-gauge railway track. A sort of miniature necropolis railway, if you will.

WHATEVER HAPPENED TO OLD LONDON BRIDGE?

There have been many London Bridges. The current, concrete span dates from only the 1970s, and replaced a 19th-century bridge that was famously sold to an American businessman – much of that bridge stands to this day in Lake Havasu City, Arizona. But what of the medieval London Bridge?

Map by
KATHERINE BAXTER

This structure crossed the river between the 13th and 19th centuries. For much of its existence, what we now call Old London Bridge was overloaded with housing, shops, chapels and even a palace. Those buildings caused a supreme bottleneck. So much so that in 1722 the Lord Mayor instigated a 'keep left' rule for traffic – often said to be the origin of Britain's left-side driving.

Eventually, the buildings had to go. The antiquated aquatic village was swept away in the 1760s to create a wider roadway. The bridge itself was also not long for this world. At almost 600 years old, it was increasingly tough to maintain and its narrow arches were a major hindrance to river traffic. The whole edifice was removed and replaced between 1824 and 1831.

But where do you dump many hundreds of tons of stone? It turns out that large chunks of Old London Bridge can still be seen around the London area, while other fragments are scattered far and wide.

The stones

Much of the stonework was reportedly dumped in the river following demolition, and there are press reports of ships striking the sunken hazard. Otherwise, the medieval stone was reused in a number of properties. The most striking surviving example seems to be Ingress Abbey in Greenhithe, Kent.

Another significant lot of stone went to the Isle of Sheppey, to build the tower of Warden Church. Unfortunately, the structure fell foul of coastal erosion. What hadn't already been demolished fell into the sea about 100 years ago.

The alcoves

The best-known remnants are the pedestrian alcoves, 14 of which graced the bridge in Georgian times, after the medieval buildings had been cleared from the roadway. Two of these distinctive shelters can be found at the eastern end of Victoria Park. A third can be found in the modern London Bridge area – it's in the courtyard of Guy's Hospital, and is currently occupied by a seated statue of John Keats. A fourth, and less well-known alcove can be found in East Sheen, Richmond, where it once formed a garden decoration for a posh house (Stawell House pronounced, for some reason, as 'shawl'). The house is long gone but the alcove survives, at the southwestern end of the Courtlands Estate.

The balustrades

Other balustrades from Old London Bridge lived on a little longer. One large section was sent over to Herne Bay in Kent. The stone was removed in 1953 following storm damage, its fate unknown. Perhaps chunks live on, somewhere in a Kentish back garden.

There are rumours that further balustrades survive at Myddelton House and Gardens in Enfield, though we've been unable to verify this for ourselves. An impressive stretch can apparently be found at Gilwell Park near Chingford. These balustrades look very similar to the Herne Bay structure.

The Royal Coat of Arms

The quiet, unassuming King's Arms on Newcomen Street, Southwark, sports – appropriately – an actual set of King's arms, which adorned the southern gateway of the bridge from 1730 until demolition.

Wooden survivals

After demolition of the bridge, the wooden piers and supports were chopped up and carved into mementos. Snuff boxes were particularly popular – an internet search yields many examples. An 1857 police report details the recovery of one such snuff box, stolen by a tramp near Bedford. A few years back, a table made from the wooden piles of the medieval bridge was sold at auction. Another (or perhaps the same) was acquired by the London Museum (now Museum of London) in 1917.

Meanwhile, Fishmongers' Hall, beside the modern bridge, contains an ornate chair made from the wood of the medieval span. The nearby Watermen's Hall has to make do with a simple fragment.

Other bits and pieces

A collection of stones, thought to be from Old London Bridge, can be found in the courtyard of St Magnus the Martyr. Other stones have been incorporated into properties on Heathfield Road, Wandsworth and (reputedly) the Woodberry Down development near Stoke Newington.

There are many further, unverifiable examples. It seems that Old London Bridge is widely scattered but not entirely vanished. Perhaps one day, someone will reclaim some of that ancient material and redress the existing London Bridge with the bones of its ancestor.

ABOUT THE MAP

Along with its illustration of Old London Bridge, there's a tremendous amount of London history crammed in here – too much for us to unpack in full (though you might find a few references elsewhere in this book, if you're sharp-eyed). Shoutout to the elephants skating on the Thames in particular – a nod to London's frost fairs (look them up) as well as the Roman invasion.

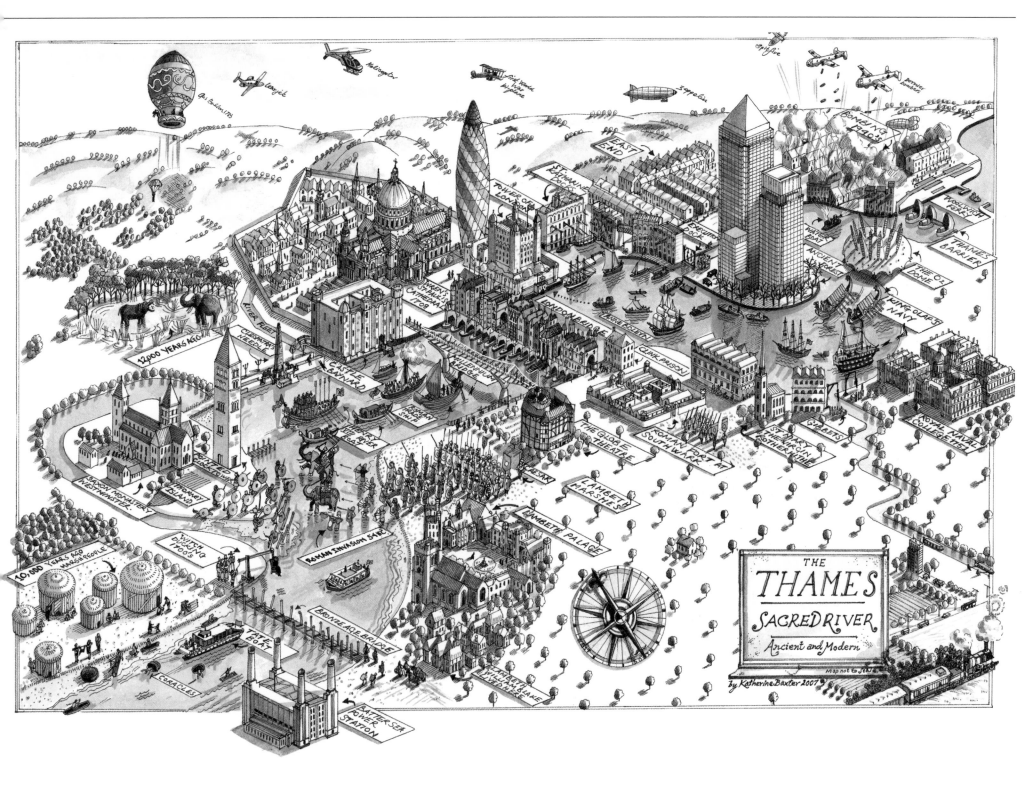

THE
THAMES
SACRED RIVER
Ancient and Modern
Map not to Scale
by Katherine Baxter 2007

GO ON A DINOSAUR HUNT IN LONDON

Whether you've got a budding paleontologist in the family, or just fancy finding out a bit more about dinosaurs, London has plenty of places where you can go properly Jurassic.

Map by
ANDY COUNCIL

Just imagine our thrill when we discovered the work of Bristol-based illustrator Andy Council, who combines architecture and dinosaurs in his illustrations. We simply had to have one of our very own.

Is this really a map? Well, as defined by the OED, a map is 'a diagrammatic representation of an area of land or sea showing physical features, cities, roads etc.', so we're going to go ahead and say yes, it is (though we don't recommend trying to use it to navigate). Whichever way you come down on that side of the argument though, it is, undeniably, cool.

So, without further ado, here is where you can find dinosaurs in London.

Natural History Museum (South Kensington)
South Kensington's Natural History Museum is the obvious go-to for dino action. Dippy, the diplodocus formerly on display in the Hintze Hall, may have packed his (or her?) bags, but the Dinosaur Gallery is still open for business.

Wander through the gallery and see the most complete stegosaurus skeleton ever found, the first T-rex fossil found, and of course, the animatronic T-rex, among plenty of other items to keep dino lovers happy.

Horniman Museum (Forest Hill)
Horniman Museum's impressive grounds are home to a Prehistoric Garden, planted with species which were around at the time dinosaurs walked the earth. Plants and trees including yew, redwood and ferns are all in there, along with a life-size sculpture of a velociraptor. Inside, the museum's Natural History Gallery has dinosaur artefacts on show.

Grant Museum of Zoology (Fitzrovia)
The Grant Museum of Zoology's impressive collection doesn't disappoint when it comes to dinosaurs. Part of an iguanodon leg bone, and bones from the spine, are on display, as well as specimens dating back to the time of the dinosaurs, including marine and flying reptiles such as ichthyosaurs and pterosaurs. The museum is also particularly proud of its collection of models of dinosaurs and other extinct species.

Crystal Palace dinosaurs
On an island in the south of Crystal Palace Park sit the Crystal Palace Park Dinosaurs, made in the 1850s and restored intermittently ever since. We hate to break it to you, but of the 29 models, only four are dinosaurs – the rest depict other prehistoric species, including mammals. If you want to start smaller, the local campsite has a model dinosaur trail for the kids.

Dinosaur crazy golf
London for some reason has multiple dino-themed crazy golf courses, perfect for family days out. Nine giant dinosaurs flank the 18 holes at Jurassic Encounter in New Malden, while Mr Mulligan's Dino Golf in Sidcup is still going strong, within a whopping 36-hole course. Over at Dinosaur Escape in Northolt, swing for your life – just avoid the questionably coloured water. Head north, meanwhile, for Jurassic Falls Adventure Golf in Walthamstow, or Dinosaur Safari Adventure Golf, Barnet.

Jamie Oliver's Diner
Jamie Oliver's Diner on Shaftesbury Avenue serves up American diner food with a side of dinosaur decor – 'dinersaur', if you will – including a giant T-rex suspended above the staircase.

Little Dinosaurs play centre
Younger dinosaur fans can get their fill at Little Dinosaurs, an indoor play centre close to Alexandra Palace with slides, climbing platforms, and squishy dinosaur mouths to climb through.

London Zoo (Regent's Park)
Crocodiles are often labelled as dinosaurs, and while this isn't correct, animals of the Crocodylia order (which includes crocodiles, alligators, caimans and gharials) are known to have outlived the dinosaurs. While we can't show you a croc which was personally around prior to the extinction of dinosaurs, we will point you in the direction of the reptile house at London Zoo, which is home to Philippine crocodiles.

ABOUT THE MAP

'My dinosaur map of London is drawn in the shape of an Iguanodon, which some of the dinosaur sculptures at Crystal Palace are based on, with the locations positioned as accurately as possible within the shape. The Natural History Museum makes up the head and the neck; the back features London Zoo, the soft play centre, The Grant Museum and Jamie's Diner. The Horniman Museum is one of the rear legs leading down to Crystal Palace park, with the crazy golf sites around the edges of the map.'
- Andy Council

10 WEIRD LONDON LAWS AND RULES

Looking into the age-old legislation of London we've uncovered many strange acts and clauses, some which still stand now and some which, sadly, are just rumours.

Map by
ANIKA MOTTERSHAW

Some of these rules and laws are so bizarre you've probably been breaking them without even knowing it (especially if you like touching pelicans).

Anyway, apparently it's a big no-no to:

1. Wear a suit of armour in Parliament
It's been illegal for MPs to enter Parliament in a suit of armour since the 1313 statute forbidding Bearing of Armour. This has never been repealed.

2. Beat a rug
You can't beat a carpet, rug or mat in the Metropolitan Police District, says Section 60 of the Metropolitan Police Act of 1839. Though it's OK to shake a doormat, as long as you get in there before 8am.

3. Take a cab if you've got the plague
Don't even think about flagging down a London cab if you've got the plague. We've got sections 33 and 34 of Public Health (Control Of Disease) Act 1984, Chapter 22 to thank for this one. The rule also applies to passengers with leprosy, rabies, food poisoning, even whooping cough – in fact, 'any notifiable diseases' – which are those you have to report to Public Health England so they can prevent a possible epidemic.

    Although it's actually alright as long as the cab driver agrees and disinfects the cab immediately afterwards.

4. Jump a queue in a tube station
Here's the most British one. We've all seen a bit of this going on, but it's actually prohibited according to TfL byelaws – as long as there's a sign or member of staff telling you not to (in this day and age no wonder so many people get away with it).

5. Slide on ice
You're not allowed to slide on ice or snow. Well, not 'in any street or other thoroughfare, to the common danger of the passengers' anyway. As far as we know, this only applies to London – so go wild in the rest of the UK.

    The law was passed as part of Section 54 of the Metropolitan Police Act Of 1839, which seems to have been a prime year for fun-sucking as they also outlawed carrying a plank (or any building materials) along a pavement.

6. Touch a pelican
Pelican-touching is 'expressly forbidden' should you happen to find one in a London park, according to the Royal Parks and Other Open Spaces Regulations 1997. You can pet one if 'prior permission is obtained'. Presumably from the park, not the pelican.

7. Dress as a Chelsea Pensioner
The myth goes that you can't don the distinctive red coat and black cap of the retired soldiers/national treasures since 1692. It's not actually illegal though; we called them and checked, and they said you could probably do it with their permission if you really wanted. We presume impersonating any other pensioner is absolutely fine.

8. Mate with the Queen's corgis
Apparently you're forbidden to allow your pet to mate with one of the Queen's corgis (though we can't find any official details of a law on the subjct). Presumably this is to avoid any unwanted mongrel offspring.

9. Fly a kite
Section 54 of our old friend the Metropolitan Police Act of 1839 states that kite flying in a public place is punishable by a fine of up to £200 if it causes 'annoyance to other people'. Mr Banks and the kids in *Mary Poppins* seem to have been completely unaware of this one.

10. Kill a swan
Though the Queen doesn't own all the breeds of swan in England, she does have first say on all mute swans (which she co-owns along with the worshipful companies of Vintners and Dyers). She's even allowed to eat them, as long as she and her diners are guests of St John's College, Cambridge. As mute swans are a protected species under the Wildlife and Countryside Act of 1981 and killing them is punishable with a £5,000 fine, we're not quite sure how this one works out. But she's obviously got a bit of money if she does need to pay up.

ABOUT THE MAP

This map comes from Anika Mottershaw, whose ambition knows no bounds. Not content with sketching one particular neighbourhood, Anika's taken the whole of Zone 1, and then some, for her hand-drawn cartography. For reasons best known to her, Bloomsbury nestles in the shadow of a giant dinosaur, Pimlico is inhabited by 'monocles and such', and Rotherhithe has a giant snail problem. Brilliant work! We've paired it here with a miscellany of equivalent London weirdness, because why not?

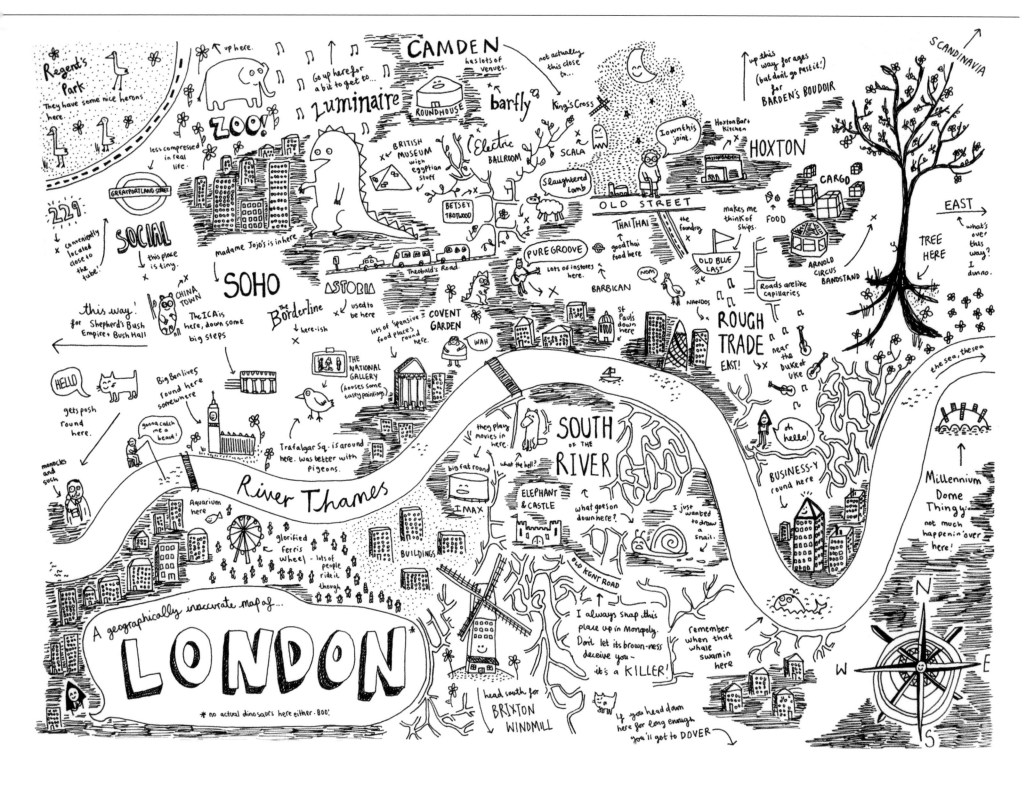

SOME OF LONDON'S BEST SECRET GARDENS

Sometimes you just want to get away from the madness of London and contemplate in peace for a while. That's where London's secret gardens come in. They're green spaces, but often surprisingly close to the busiest parts of the city – ideal for grabbing a few minutes of respite before getting back to it.

Map by
JANINA SCHRÖTER

Museum of Brands Café

Kiwis are being grown in London. Or at least they are in the summer, at the Museum of Brands' café garden in Ladbroke Grove. It's worth visiting even if you're not going to the museum.

SOAS Japanese Roof Garden

Tucked away on a roof off the western corner of Russell Square is a small, but perfectly formed, Japanese garden (above the Brunei Gallery at SOAS to be precise). It's enclosed on all sides (though you can peek at people by people in an office on one side – and be peeked at in return), with a little raked gravel section and wisteria hanging above benches in spring. Yep, we like wisteria.

The Phoenix Garden

This little slice of greenery is not what you'd expect to find between Covent Garden and Tottenham Court Road, but there it is – bristling with roses, daisies, banana palms – and all manner of wildlife (it's great for dragonflies in summer). It receives no council funding so relies on public donations to stay open. Keep an eye out for frogs too.

Ravenscourt Park Walled Garden

Hammersmith has its own secret spot in the form of Ravenscourt Park Walled Garden, in the northeast of the park. It's run by volunteers, so if you're looking to get hands-on with a green-fingered project, this may be one for you.

St Dunstan in the East

Not far from the river between Monument and the Tower of London is St Dunstan in the East, a bombed-out church in the City, now with garden benches. It can get busy with lunching City workers, but the rest of the time it feels impressively secluded.

St John's Lodge Gardens

We found this one once, completely by accident, then struggled to find it again for years – most Regent's Park visitors head for Queen Mary's Rose Gardens instead. But persist and you'll find St John's Lodge Gardens. Designed by Robert Weir Shultz in 1889 as a series of compartments ornamented with sculpture and stonework, the gardens were intended to be 'fit for meditation'. Hopefully you'll find peace here.

Rembrandt Gardens

One for the boat lovers among you; Rembrandt Gardens overlook Little Venice in Paddington, where Regent's Canal meets Grand Union Canal. Seats overlook the water, among lawns and tulip borders (a nod, we assume, to the Dutch artist after whom this place is named).

Gibbon's Rent

If you ever need somewhere quiet to sit down between the craziness of London Bridge station and Tooley Street, slip into Gibbon's Rent. The Shard towering over you won't allow you to forget that you're in central London, but provided you don't visit at a lunchtime in the summer, you should be able to bag yourself a seat… and even a book from the mini lending library.

Marococo

We've never been to this one, but heck are we intrigued by it. Behind the Belgravia branch of Rococo chocolatier is a Moroccan-style garden, cleverly named Marococo, with potted plants, Moroccan tiles, and a fountain. Lovely.

Postman's Park

Another favourite lunch spot for nearby office workers, Postman's Park is home to the Watts Memorial which celebrates 'heroism in every-day life'. It's also littered with benches for those looking for somewhere to tuck into their sarnies, as well as paved paths and flower beds. It's also probably the least-secret garden on our list.

Christchurch Greyfriars

Not far from Postman's Park is Christchurch Greyfriars Church Garden, overshadowed by the church tower. The church itself was destroyed in World War II, but wooden towers representing the pillars which once held up the roof are now adorned with climbing roses and clematis.

Chelsea Physic Garden

How does a secret garden next to the Thames sound? Chelsea Physic Garden is one for those with serious horticultural interests, focusing on edible and medicinal plants, with 5,000 species on display. If you're just looking for somewhere a bit more peaceful than King's Road, that's okay too.

Barbican Conservatory

Among the brutalist architecture of the Barbican estate lies a steamy oasis, flush with palms and tropical blooms. It claims to be the second biggest conservatory in London (Kew taking top prize), and is home to 2,000 tropical plant species. Two ponds include some impressively fat carp, and a group of terrapins that had to be removed from Hampstead Heath ponds after terrorising the local native wildlife.

ABOUT THE MAP

Don't let the giant buildings fool you; there's quite a lot of London packed into this bespoke map from artist Janina Schröter, which stretches from London Bridge all the way out to Hammersmith. We particularly loved how the bright colours of the gardens pop against her quirky black-and-white illustrations.

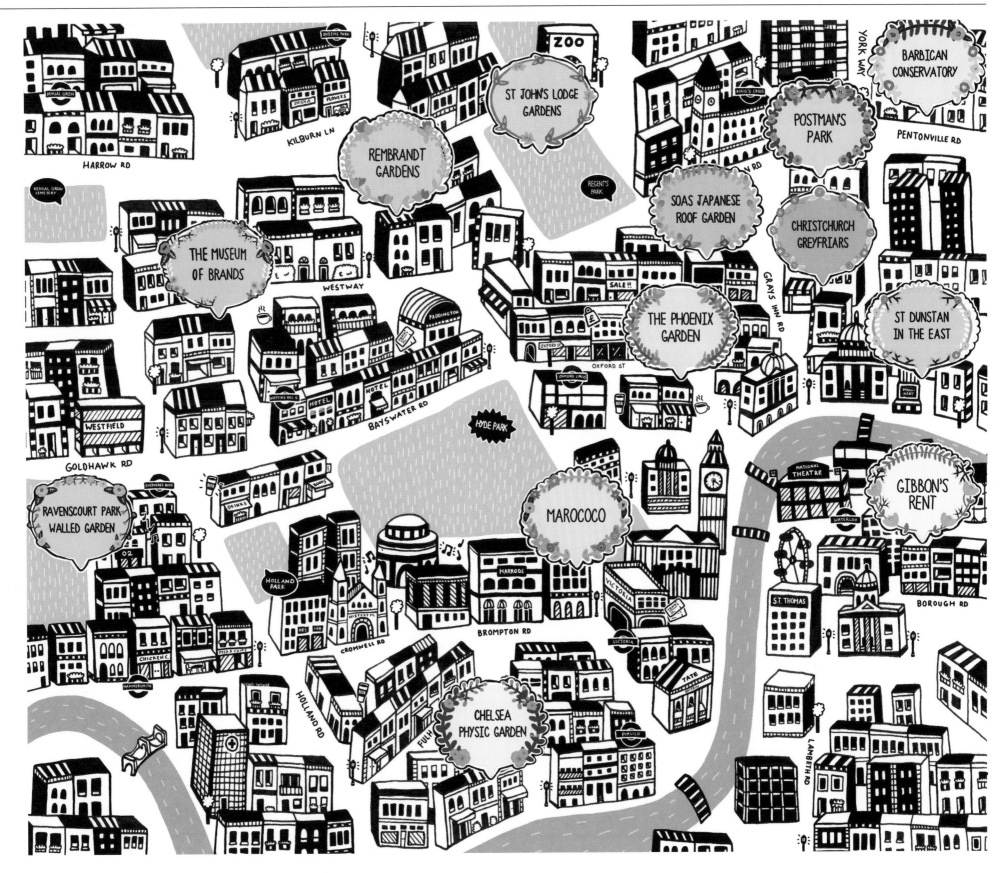

LONDON'S LOST VICTORIAN BUILDINGS

The Victorian Society has compiled a list of the less well-known Victorian buildings London should never have lost.

Map by
Bek Cruddace

Euston station

The Victorian Society's battle to save the Euston Arch is famous, but most haven't heard of the stunning interior of the 1849 Euston station, which had a similar feel to Grand Central Station in New York.

Royal Doulton Factory

The main Royal Doulton building on the Thames in Lambeth was a tour-de-force of what the company could offer in architectural terracotta and tiles. While the main building was pulled down in the 1950s due to war damage, a small part remains (and is now listed) to give a tantalising glimpse of what has been lost.

The London Coal Exchange

Opened by Prince Albert on 30 October 1849, this was one of the first substantial cast iron buildings, predating the hall at the Great Exhibition. The Grade II-listed building was demolished in 1962 to allow road widening, but in one sense it lives on – its decorations are the model for the City of London's dragon boundary markers.

No. 1 Poultry

Many assume that the postmodern building opposite the Royal Exchange replaced something destroyed by bomb damage. In fact, the listed Victorian building was destroyed in the 1990s after three public inquiries, and even the intervention of the House of Lords.

Royal Aquarium

It's odd to think that opposite Westminster Abbey there was once a pleasure palace hosting variety acts and a music hall. The 1876 aquarium with attached theatre had a main hall 340ft long, covered with a glass and iron roof and decorated with palm trees, fountains, sculpture and 13 large tanks meant to be filled with sea creatures. The Methodist Central Hall was built on the site in 1911.

St Thomas's Hospital

St Thomas's Hospital was rebuilt in 1868 by Henry Currey to a design showing the influence of Florence Nightingale's ideas on the free flowing of air, and the isolation of patients. It was extensively damaged in World War II and most of the original blocks have been demolished with little to suggest the once-impressive river frontage opposite the Houses of Parliament.

Imperial Institute

South Kensington once had another imposing building among the ranks of the Natural History Museum, the V&A and the Science Museum. The University of London demolished the main buildings but saved the tower after much public outcry.

Columbia Market, Bethnal Green

If you were to mention Columbia Market today most people would assume you were talking about the flower market. Yet the road was once graced with a huge gothic market of 1869 designed by Henry Darbyshire. It lasted just 16 years, and closed in 1885.

Hotel Cecil

Like the Savoy, the Hotel Cecil opened off the Strand and stretched down to the river. On opening in 1896 it was said to be the largest hotel in the world with 1,000 rooms. It closed in 1930 and was demolished in just six weeks to be replaced with Shell-Mex House.

Museum of Practical Geology

Designed by the Crown Architect James Pennethorne and opened by Prince Albert in 1851, the Museum was one of the first great national museums. Its collections included the stone samples made for the construction of the Palace of Westminster. The museum moved to South Kensington and the building was demolished in 1936.

Birkbeck Bank

This was not your average Victorian bank. Opened in 1902, it had a bigger hall than the Bank of England – 72ft across – and was surmounted by a cast iron dome. The hall was lined with Doulton terracotta and decorated with tiles, 16 murals, stained glass and elaborate ironwork. Birkbeck Bank was demolished in 1965 after an appeal failed to save it.

Gerrard Street telephone exchange

This Elizabethan-Edwardian style building, designed by Leonard Stokes, was one of London's first purpose-built telephone exchanges. The building was meant to demonstrate ideas for 'the logical architectural treatment of a steel framed commercial structure'. Perhaps today's architects could be a bit more creative with their treatments for such buildings?

ABOUT THE MAP

We posed quite a challenge to Bek Cruddace when we came to her with this idea: accurately illustrate a bunch of buildings that don't exist any more. A fair amount of research (thank you, Victorian Society) later, though, and voila!

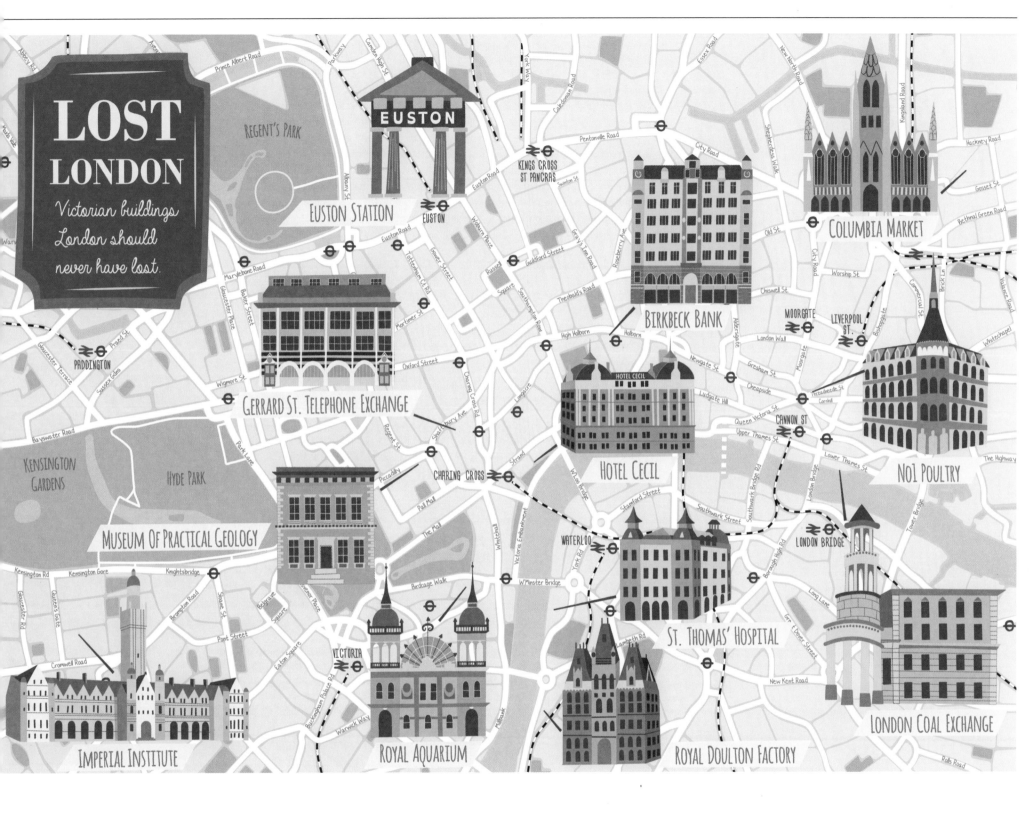

LOST LONDON

Victorian buildings London should never have lost.

EUSTON STATION

GERRARD ST. TELEPHONE EXCHANGE

MUSEUM OF PRACTICAL GEOLOGY

IMPERIAL INSTITUTE

ROYAL AQUARIUM

BIRKBECK BANK

COLUMBIA MARKET

HOTEL CECIL

No1 POULTRY

St. THOMAS' HOSPITAL

ROYAL DOULTON FACTORY

LONDON COAL EXCHANGE

9 REALLY TERRIBLE JOKES ABOUT LONDON

If Londonist *were ever to make a box of Christmas crackers, these are the rubbish jokes we would fill them with. Enjoy.*

ABOUT THE MAP

To accompany our dreadful London jokes – some truly majestic puns from London design studio Heretic. If Places Were Faces is a glorious tour de force of celebrity punnery, and we heartily recommend checking out the larger work to see all the bits that we couldn't fit on the page. Alan Rickmansworth, anyone?

'My mum bought most of my presents from the London Borough of Hounslow.'
'Feltham?'
'No, I don't want to spoil the surprise.'

What's the difference between a south London football supporter and a plasterer?
One's a Millwall fan, the other's a fill-wall man.

Prehistoric Londoner 1: 'I just fired an arrow into the mouth of the River Lea.'
Prehistoric Londoner 2: 'Bow Creek?'
Prehistoric Londoner 1: 'No, it's made from the finest yew wood, and never makes a sound.'

Knock Knock
'Who's there?'
'Your neighbour…'
'Look mate, this is London. I don't want to know you. I will only acknowledge you if you play your tunes too loud, and then I'm calling the police. OK?'

Why did the chicken cross the North Circular Road?
To get from Finchley to Hendon.

'Speaking of chickens, a gang of them recently attacked my friends in south London.'
'Peckham?'
'Ah, I'm going to have to stop you there. This joke is too obvious.'

'I'm getting a nasty rash from this sweater I picked up in southeast London.'
'Woolwich?'
'It can't be that. It's made from polyester.'

'Did you hear about the punster who was arrested in Hackney last night?'
'Yeah, bit of a Mare, that one.'
'The handcuffs were Clapton.'
'I guess the police were at the end of the Wick.'
'At least they managed to Shacklewell.'

And finally, an old classic:
Why did Sherlock Holmes measure the Monopoly board?
To see if the game was a foot.

Map by
Jon Rundall and Luke Frost

ALAN RICKMANSWORTH

HAROLD PINNER

MIA HARROW

THE EDGEW[...]

WOODY HAR[...]

GRAYSON PERIVALE

ACTON KUTCHE[...]

NEVILLE SOUTHALL

ISAAC HAYES

DAVID BRENTFORD

KEW TIP GARDENS

CHARLIE EASTS[...]

ADRIAN MOLESEY

TEDDINGTON SHERINGHAM

MARTIN LUTHER KINGSTON

JONATHAN RICHMOND

EWELL BRYN[...]

COLIN DALE
TIM HENDON
MUHAMMAD ALI PALLY
TURNPIKE TOM VERLAINE
NOEL EDMONTON
SEVEN SISTERS OF MERCY
DAVID LEE VALLEY ROTH
RONNIE WOODFORD
HUGH GANTS HILL
TED HAMPSTEAD HEATH
PETER CROUCH END
DAMON STAMFORD HILL
WALTHAMSTOW VILLAGE PEOPLE
NEASDEN
PHIL TUFNELL PARK
CHUCK
BILLIE HOLLOWAY
DUSTY SPRINGFIELD PARK
OLIVIA STOKE NEWINGTON JOHN
ERIC CLAPTON
LEYTON HEWITT
UPTON PARK JI-SUNG
RONNIE BARKING
CANONBURY
HOBSON GREEN LANES
RIDLEY SCOTT ROAD MARKET
SHEENA EAST HAM
KEVIN KILBURN
PETE KENTISH TOWNSHEND
DAVID ESSEX ROAD
VALLE BERRY & ISLINGTON
DALSTON HOFFMAN
CAMDEN DIAZ
JACK WHITE CITY
THE ST TRAIN'S WOOD
DAVID LA CHAPEL MARKET
MONEY SOHO
HACKNEY WICK ROSS
FELICITY KENSAL RISE
WHITNEY EUSTON
ANDY SUMMERSTOWN
ANGEL-X-MURRAY
EXMOUTH MARKY MARKET
GEORGE MICHAEL SHOREDITCH
NOEL LONDON FIELDINGS
DAVID HACKNEY
BOW DEREK
PAUL NEWHAM
CYBILL SHEPHERD'S BUSH
JOOLS HOLLAND PARK
TIMMY NOTTING HILL
BURT LANCASTER GATE
GINGER BAKER STREET
BOB MARYLEBO
PICCADILLY PARTON
DON KING'S CROSS
DICKY HATTON GARDEN
JOHN COOKE CLERKENWELL
MARK X AMESBURY
SAMP BRIXTON
MARIO BISHOPS GATE
BRICK LANE EKLAND
WALTER WHITE CHAPEL
BERNARD CANNING TOWN
BRIAN WOOLWICH FERRY
JEFFREY MARBLE ARCHER
IAN DRURY LANE
RAY BARBICAN
ROGER MOORGATE
GARY ALDGATE
JO STRAND
RU ST PAULS
HANK I MOON
PHIL SILVERS TOWN
HIGH ST KEN LOACH
CHRISSIE HYDE PARK
EARL'S COURT SWEATSHIRT
LINDSEY BUCKINGHAM PALACE
SHIRLEY TEMPLE
BRADY MAYFAIR
BARRY WHITEHALL
WILLIAM BOROUGH
THE SHARDE
ROGER CANADA WATER
ISLE OF SNOOP DOGGS
THAMES BARRIER McGUIGEN
IHAM GREEN
MC HAMMERSMITH
GRAM PARSON'S GREEN
CHELSEA CLINTON
MICHAEL KNIGHTS
ULTRAVAUX HALL
WATERLOU REED
ROY ELEPHANT & CASTLE
TIM BURGESS PARK
MICHAEL ROTHERHITHE
STEPHEN NEW CROSS GATES
CHARLTON
BLACK HEATH LEDGER
PAUL WELLING
E MORTLAKE
JOHN BARNES
LES BATTERSEA
ROBERT NINE ELMS LANE
EDDY KENNINGTON
KEITH HARRIS & OVAL
LAMBETH DITTO
VICTORIA PECKHAM
TALKING NUNHEYDS
JOHNNY DEPTFORD
ELTHAM JOHN
ERITH PIAF
WILLIAM WANDSWORTH
ORSON STOCKWELLES
TONI BRIXTON
PECKHAM RYE COODER
HUEY LEWISHAM
BRUCE LEE GREEN
JOHN MOTTINGHAM
CLAPHAM AYRES
TOOTING BECK
CAROLINE A HERNE HILL
KELLY LE BROCKLEY
BILLY CRYSTAL PALACE
SYDENHAM BARRETT
FORREST GUMP HILL
CATFORD DEELEY
CHEVY WIMBLEDON CHASE
TOOTING BROADWAY AND THE MAYTALS
MICHAELA STREATHAM
BORIS BECKENHAM
STEVE SIDCUP
PAUL MERTON
MORDEN HARKET
COLLIERS WOODY ALLEN
BILLY BOB THORNTON HEATH
SEAN PENGE
NICK CHISTLEHURST CAVE
ROY ORPINGTON

A BANKER'S PUB CRAWL

The City of London: home to bankers and architecturally fascinating pubs – many of which used to be banks. These days, they're where the bankers go to celebrate their bonuses. Put on your whistle, pick up your briefcase – we're going on a banker's pub crawl of London.

Map by
Tom Woolley Illustration

The Knights Templar

Catch the tube (or if you want to be properly banker-like, a cab) to Chancery Lane for our first stop, The Knights Templar. Now part of the Wetherspoon chain, this grand building used to be owned by Union Bank. Although a former banking house, it's named after a medieval order that established the nearby Inner and Middle Temples.

With a vast bar and tables scattered everywhere, you're pretty much guaranteed a seat downstairs. For something cosier, go upstairs, which is full of niches, smaller rooms and a balcony. The selection of beers is as wide-ranging as at any Wetherspoon and updated constantly. You won't need a banker's salary to afford one, either.

After having your fill, take a short walk south down to The Old Bank of England – housed in the Bank of England's former law courts.

The Old Bank of England

The interior of this place could easily win some prize for most elaborate decor in a pub. Its incredibly high, extravagantly decorated ceilings are adorned with massive chandeliers hanging above the huge wooden bar in the centre of the hall.

Comfy leather sofas are dotted around but if you fancy a bird's-eye view of the hall, head up the twisting staircase to the mezzanine. It's a Fuller's pub, so it'd be rude not to have a London Pride.

After our first couple of drinks in two cavernous watering holes, let's head along Fleet Street to the very different Ye Olde Cheshire Cheese.

Ye Olde Cheshire Cheese

This mazy pub is across four floors and, although not a former bank, has been a favourite with bankers and City workers for decades. In 1962, the pub gave the Museum of London a number of erotic plaster-of-Paris tiles found in the upstairs room, suggesting the higher levels used to be used as a brothel. It's now a Samuel Smith's pub; the beer selection is cheap though not particularly inspiring. A good spot for an affordable G&T, we reckon.

Next, stagger up Ludgate Hill, past St Paul's Cathedral and take a left at Bow Lane to Williamson's Tavern.

Williamson's Tavern

A former residence of the Lord Mayor of London, the intricate gates at the entrance of this pub were gifted by William III, who dined there whilst it was still the mayor's home. It became a hotel when the mayor decided it wasn't a grand enough residence, and then a pub in the early 20th century. There's a good selection of traditional ales on the bar as well as craft beers, and they have a fondness for good gin too. Or you might decide it's time for a sensible soft drink.

Next, turn left up Bow Lane and then take a right along Cheapside to 1 Lombard Street.

1 Lombard Street

This former bank has been turned into a high-class brasserie and bar. The neo-classical interior is striking, with an oval-shaped bar under a huge glass-domed skylight. It's rather modern compared to the other stops, and fancier too. Splash out on one of their espresso martinis for a little pick-me-up.

When you're ready to go back to the pints, cross the road along Lombard Street then turn left at Gracechurch Street, and to our penultimate stop, The Crosse Keys.

The Crosse Keys

Another Wetherspoon and former banking hall, the huge marble pillars and grand circular bar make this pub yet another stunner (just excuse the menus offering beer and burger deals). It's so big you won't have trouble finding a seat, but again it's quieter upstairs: go to the balcony where there are plenty of nooks and crannies (and you can pretend to chat about secretive banker stuff).

Just two minutes north along Cornhill is our final stop and another Fuller's pub, The Counting House.

The Counting House

This former banking house was built in 1893 and still has plenty of its original fixtures and fittings. The dark wood-panelled walls and bar combined with the slightly ostentatious skylight and mezzanine floor make it quite a spot for a pint.

The clientele is, unsurprisingly, mostly bankers and their clients – making this the most banker-like stop on the crawl and the ideal place to while the rest of the night away, assuming you haven't seen enough ales. Or suits, for that matter.

ABOUT THE MAP

Please don't tear this page out to take with you on your pub crawl, however tempting that sounds – it was drawn by Tom Woolley especially for us, and we rather like it.
Also: please drink responsibly!

CHANCERY LANE

THE KNIGHTS TEMPLAR

CHANCERY LA

START

CAREY ST

YE OLDE CHESHIRE CHEESE

FLEET ST

THE OLD BANK OF ENGLAND

TUDOR ST

RIVER THAMES

FARRINGDON ST

ST PAUL'S CATHEDRAL

ST PAUL'S

LUDGATE HILL

QUEEN VICTORIA ST

BLACKFRIARS

BLACKFRIARS BRIDGE

WILLIAMSON'S TAVERN

CHEAPSIDE

BANK

1 LOMBARD STREET

SOUTHWARK BRIDGE

LOWER THAMES ST

MOORGATE

THE COUNTING HOUSE

FINISH

CORNHILL

KING WILLIAM ST

MONUMENT

GRACECHURCH ST

THE CROSSE KEYS

'HOW DO YOU SAY...?': AN INCOMPLETE GUIDE

We've all heard it. 'Can you tell me where Lie-sester Square is?'. English place names can be a bit of a challenge to the outsider.

Even longtime Londoners might struggle with some pronunciations. Hands up who's contemplated the correct way to say 'Theydon Bois'? Here's a quick guide to some of the commonest tongue-puzzlers:

Cadogan Square/Hall

The Cadogan name is all over the Sloane Square area, named after a Georgian noble whose family still own much of the land thereabouts. It should be pronounced as Ca-duggan, not Cad-ogan.

Deptford

The case of the silent 'p'. Simply, 'Det-ford'.

Greenwich/Southwark/Woolwich/Chiswick

The 'silent w' is a common peril for non-natives. The phenomenon tends to crop up in names of Anglo Saxon origin. If you see a W in the middle of a place name, just ignore it (hence Gren-itch, Suth-urk, Wool-itch and Chis-ick). It's only a rule of thumb, though. Don't try it with Holloway or Queensway.

Hainault

On the Central Line, it seems that pronouncing words the French way is passé. A few stops round from Theydon Bois, we find Hainault, which is enunciated as Hay-nolt rather than the Gallic 'ay-no'.

Holborn

A perennial puzzler, Holborn is best pronounced using as few letters as possible – o'b'n rather than Hole-born. Ho-bun is probably the commonest form among locals.

Homerton

The Simpsons fans might be tempted towards Homer-tun, but the correct form is more like Hommer-tun.

Leicester Square

Any native knows this is pronounced 'Less-ter', but that complex run of vowels commonly stumps visitors.

The Mall

Potentially confusing for North American visitors, who may be expecting a shopping centre. The 'a' is short, making the word rhyme with 'pal'. And, as it happens, the name was borrowed from the neighbouring Pall Mall (definitely not pronounced Paul Maul), which itself was called after a croquet-like game called Pell Mell.

Marylebone

As with Holborn, using fewer letters gets you nearer to the local pronunciation (up to a point). Mar'l'bun is a good start. Marry-lebone seems commonplace. Mary-le-bone is the tourist's choice, and close to the historical roots in St Mary-le-Bourne church.

Penge

It rhymes with 'henge'.

Plaistow

The correct form is 'Plass-tow'.

Rotherhithe

This had never struck us as particularly tricky, until one (anonymous) *Londonist* contributor admitted: 'This probably marks me out as a moron, but I was convinced Rotherhithe was pronounced Rotherhither when I first moved to London. If we were in Germany, I'd totally have been right.'

Ruislip

We're advised that this should be pronounced 'Rye-slip'.

Theydon Bois

A bit of a teaser, even for locals. The consensus seems to be 'Theydon Boyce' (or Boyz), given credence by tube stop announcements. But we've found several reports of bus drivers pronouncing it as Theydon Boy. Most definitely, it's not Theydon Bwahh.

Tottenham

Most Londoners probably say something like Tott-num. The name was most famously mangled by former Spurs midfielder Osvaldo 'Ossie' Ardiles, who rolled it out to 'Tottingham' in 'Ossie's Dream', the top-10 hit from Chas & Dave.

ABOUT THE MAP

We like the way all the different London locations on Ursula's map go sprawling into one another – it feels very in keeping with the spirit of London. We have a feeling we'll be staring at this one for hours.

Map by
Ursula Hitz

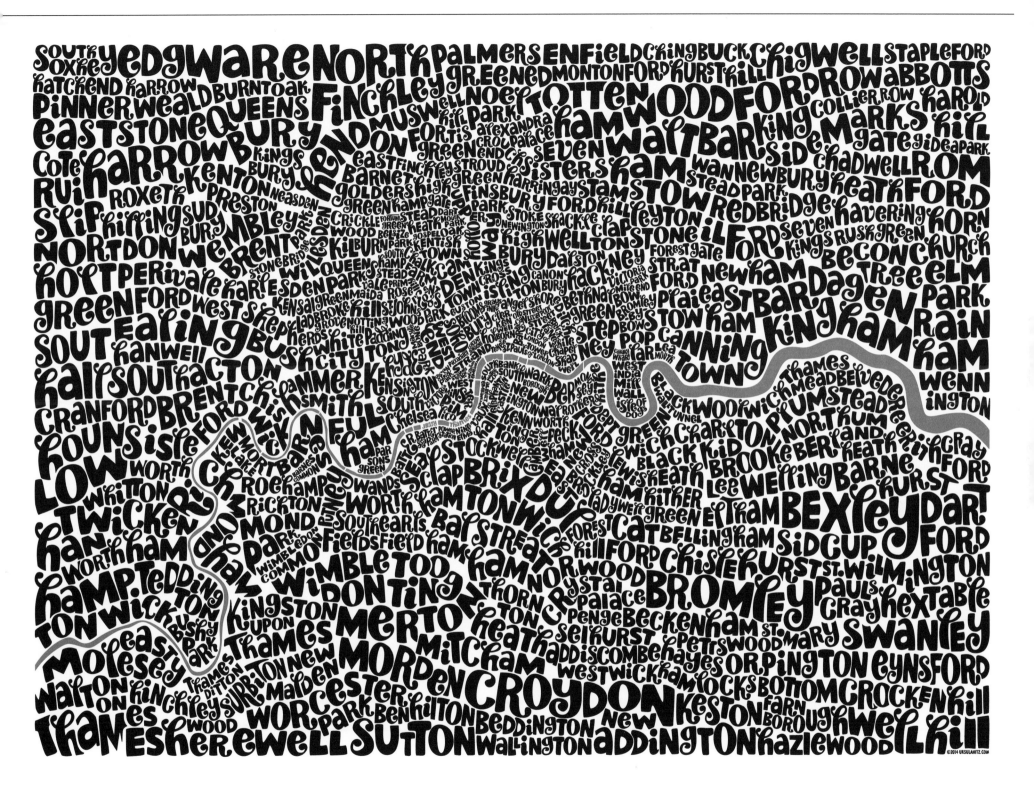

THINGS YOU MIGHT NOT KNOW ABOUT SOUTH LONDON

Unlike its northern counterpart, south London is famously poorly served by tube links (though the Overground and DLR go some way towards making up for that). It's nice down here though: plenty of commons and parks, and a surprising amount of things to do.

Map by
TILLY AKA RUNNING FOR CRAYONS

The Shard isn't the UK's tallest structure

The Shard is, without argument, the tallest building in London. You might assume that it's the tallest structure in the country. It's not – nine communications masts around the country are taller. The Shard stands 309.6m to its tip, making it the tallest building in the UK. But there's a difference between buildings and structures – and the UK's tallest structure is the Skelton Mast in Cumbria at 365m high. Even that pales in comparison to the former record-holder. The Belmont Mast in Lincolnshire once stood 387.7m tall – higher than the roof (though not the spire) of New York's Empire State Building. It has since been reduced to around 352m, which is still much taller than the Shard.

There's no wheel on the bridge of the HMS *Belfast*

There are plenty of instruments on the bridge of the *Belfast*, but there doesn't seem to be any way to steer the boat. This is because the bridge provides the Captain with a great view of the battle but is also the easiest part of the ship to target. And the last thing a ship needs is to lose steering in the heat of a battle. So the actual wheel and controls are located deep in the protected interior of the *Belfast* and orders are relayed from the bridge.

Old Kent Road is the only Monopoly property located south of the river

Nothing more to say about that really – Whitechapel is likewise the only east London property on a board heavily skewed to central London.

Vauxhall: home of astronauts

The British Interplanetary Society, just five minutes' walk from Vauxhall station, was founded in 1933. Its aim was simple: get people into space. In its earliest days, the society put forward plans to reach the Moon. A 1930s design for a lunar module hangs proudly in the society's hallway. It shares many similarities with the landers that NASA eventually sent to the Moon three decades later.

Vauxhall has other aerospace connections. During the 19th century, the area was synonymous with balloon flights, the most advanced aerial technology of the day.

Part of Peckham was almost obliterated for the Channel Tunnel

When the Channel Tunnel got the green light in 1987, British Rail announced its preferred route into London – entering a tunnel at the southeastern fringes of the capital with Waterloo as its primary terminal. Warwick Gardens, a small park just west of Peckham Rye station, was to be the location of the junction where trains bound for Waterloo would leave the tunnel and join the existing domestic lines. Warwick Gardens would have to be dug up to construct the sub-surface junction, while the nearby Holly Grove conservation area of attractive Georgian and Victorian housing would have become a major junction of the rail link. British Rail compulsory purchased over 100 properties in the immediate area.

Peckham found itself an unlikely saviour. In 1991, with a general election looming, senior Tory MPs became worried that a southerly route for the high-speed link could cost them seats in southeast London and Kent. They backed an eastern route instead; the rest is history.

Brixton has its own currency

Market Row in Brixton boasts the world's first local currency cash point, dispensing the Brixton Pound (B£), which can be spent in more than 300 independent businesses in the area. The rather funky B£ notes feature local celebrities including David Bowie and Luol Deng, as well as some public art from the area.

There's a reason the Old Royal Naval College has a gap in it

Christopher Wren's distinctive double-wing design for the ORNC wasn't just a curious whim. When the great architect was working on the new building, Queen Mary requested that the unobstructed view from the Queen's House to the Thames was preserved. When royalty requests, one tends to oblige, hence the gap.

Blackheath might be London's true home of sport

Wimbledon, Wembley, Twickenham and Lord's; London's celebrated homes of sport. But for those searching for the real home of London sport, Blackheath is arguably the place to start. The pasture gave birth to the world's first independent rugby and hockey clubs, the first golf club south of the Scottish border and three of the eleven founder members of the Football Association.

There are tunnels underneath the Thames Barrier

Two tunnels directly beneath the Thames Barrier are used by maintenance teams to move quickly from pier to pier – as well as for training by the emergency services.

These are uniquely sensorial tunnels. A faint, musty odour pervades the air. Voices echo from unseen parts of the structure. A ship passes overhead, and the hum of its engines permeates down to this riverbed subway. Colour-coded pipes and conduits lace around bulkheads. A walk beneath the Thames Barrier is truly atmospheric.

ABOUT THE MAP

We loved the different tribes of Londoners populating this 'sarf of the river' map, as explained by its creator Tilly: 'Along with plotting the well known landmarks I focused on the different types of people and fashion you can find in that area of London which is always my favourite part of creating any map'. We hope there are a few Londonists among them as well.

OXO TOWER

THE SHARD

HMS Belfast

CANARY WHARF

LONDON EYE

LONDON Aquarium

FLORENCE Nightingale Museum

CITY HALL

MUDCHUTE Park & Farm

THE O2

THAMES BARRIER

IMPERIAL WAR MUSEUM

DESIGN MUSEUM

Lower Rd

ISLE OF Dogs

Woolwich Rd

Old Kent Rd

Cutty Sark

GREENWICH MARKET

ROYAL ARTILLERY MUSEUM

THE OVAL

PECKHAM

QUEEN'S HOUSE

VAUXHALL

THE FAN MUSEUM

Greenwich mean Time

Shooters Hill Rd

HERNE HILL VELODROME

BRIXTON

Lordship Lane

DULWICH VILLAGE

Brownhill Rd

Blackheath Village

SOUTH EAST LONDON

VOLCANO

WAYS TO TELL WHEN YOU'VE BECOME A REAL LONDONER

So you own a book of London maps, you've beefed up on city trivia, and you know how to pronounce Theydon Bois. Congratulations, you can now call yourself a Londonist.

Map by
HOUSE OF CALLY

A Londoner, however, is another thing altogether. It's not enough just to live here; it's a rite of passage. Here's our list of what it takes to be a real Londoner…

Try to be clever to avoid a public transport snafu and still get caught out

Signalling problems on the Central line? No problem: you don't need Citymapper to work out an alternative route – you're a real Londoner. You deftly swerve away from the station entrance (you're so real you don't even need to approach the barriers to know there's a problem), jumping on a bus that will connect you to your destination. Except then the bus breaks down. Congratulations: now you're a real Londoner.

See Will Self

Will Self is our Woody Allen. If you haven't seen him on one of his regular perambulations, you'll see him in the pub or perhaps a Pret. Do not, however, engage him in conversation unless you have a dictionary handy.

Have a close encounter with a tube mouse

We don't mean 'see one on the tracks'. Any tourist can do that. We're talking about having one run across your foot as it emerges from a hole in the wall next to where you're standing; we once heard of a friend of a friend who had one disappear up his trouser leg. Extra London points if you don't squeal like a small child during your close encounter of the furry kind.

'Sarf of the river? At this time of night?'

It's a cliché about cabbies not wanting to venture into the mean streets of Wandsworth or Nunhead after midnight, and it's a cliché largely because it doesn't happen often. But it does happen. It's particularly annoying when the cab's gone 30 metres and hit an inexplicable wall of traffic and the driver's clearly thought 'bugger this'.

A fiver no longer seems extortionate for a pint

Paying a fiver for a pint, sadly, isn't that uncommon anymore. The real Londoner doesn't make a fuss about this. The real Londoner suppresses a wince and vows to switch to drinking bitter.

ABOUT THE MAP

This map is the result of five months of work by artist Cally Lathey, and features both tourist hotspots and lesser-known sights. Cultural icons including the Royal Vauxhall Tavern, Union Chapel in Islington and Hackney Empire all feature, and we love the colourful doodles such as the ballet shoes at Sadler's Wells and the peacocks in Holland Park.

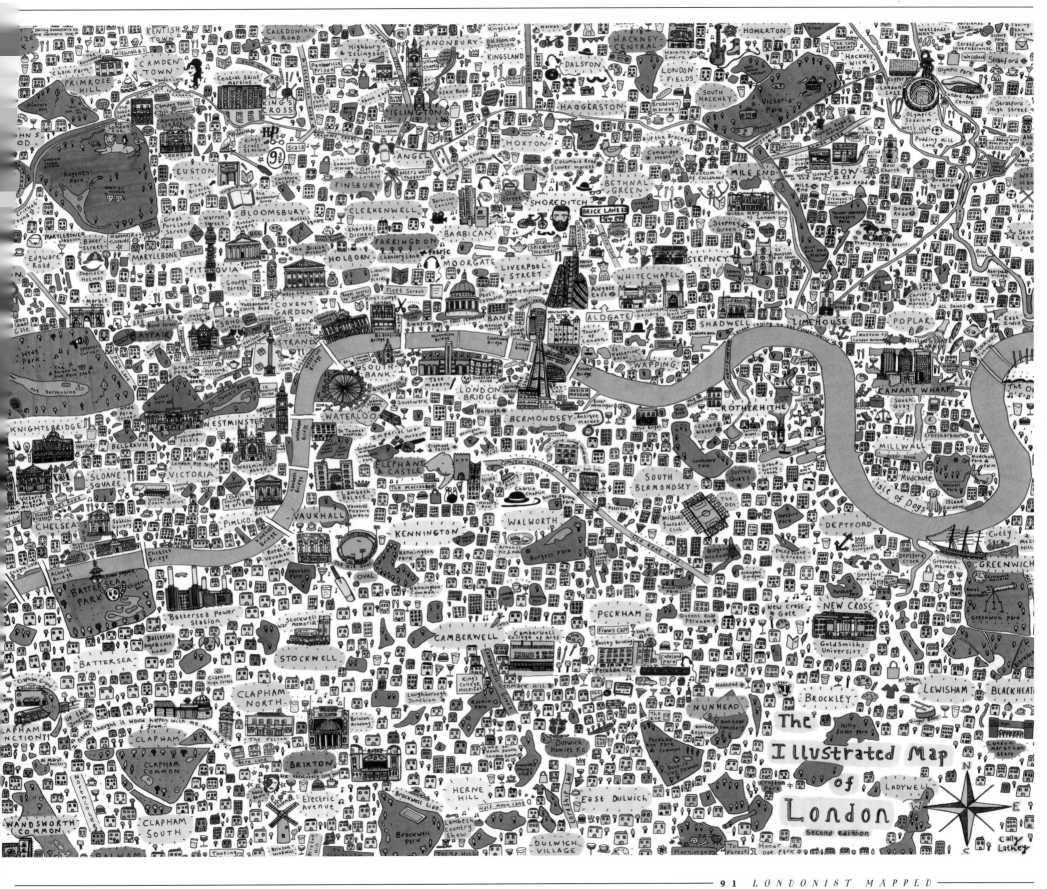

ABOUT THE ARTISTS

Luke Agbaimoni
tubemapper.com 🐦 @tubemapper

Luke Agbaimoni is a London-based digital photographer and designer. He has an arts background with a degree in graphic design. Luke has a special love for dusk and night photography, enjoying the technical challenge of capturing low light images.

Katherine Baxter
katherinebaxter.com 🐦 @baxillustrate

Katherine Baxter lives in London and hand-draws her maps using traditional methods – her trusty rotring pens are her constant companions. She is commissioned not simply for her drawing, but her creative and narrative ability to interpret a brief beyond the basic product of cartography; her main aim is to create something beautiful that is informative in nature. The London Parks map was originally created for londontown.com.

Hartwig Braun
hartwigbraun.com 🐦 @hartwigbraun

Hartwig Braun is a fine artist specialising in design-led illustrative works, using his architectural background to create expansive, detailed and engaging cityscapes utilising a mixture of organic materials and digital methods.

Amy Charlotte Bridges
etsy.com/uk/shop/AmyCharlotteShop
🐦 @ACillustrator

Amy Charlotte is a London-based illustrator specialising in highly detailed hand-drawn maps drawn directly onto paper with a fine line pen. She successfully captures the atmosphere, people, architecture and history of each area.

Matt Brown/Londonist
Londonist.com 🐦 @mattfromlondon

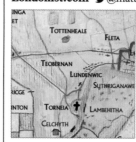

Matt (known as M@) is former editor of Londonist and author of several books about the capital. His maps have featured in the national press. Further Anglo-Saxon maps by Matt appear in Patricia Bracewell's Emma of Normandy novels.

Lucie Conoley Illustration
lucieconoley.com 🐦 @LucieConoley

Lucie Conoley is an artist/illustrator based in West Sussex. She creates bespoke maps in various mediums under the name of 'The Mips' –The Most Important Places – detailing all the individual places that build the unique character of each area.

Andy Council
andycouncil.co.uk 🐦 @AndyCouncil

Andy Council is a Bristol-based artist who creates composite beasts made up of architectural landmarks and other recognisable elements. His work takes the form of illustration, painting and huge murals which can be seen across the UK.

Bek Cruddace
bekcruddace.co.uk 🐦 @bekcruddace

Bek Cruddace is a designer and illustrator based in Hampshire who specialises in illustrated maps. Since 2011 Bek has built up a solid client base with many return and long-term clients combined with private commissions and her own retail designs.

Francisco Dans

http://francisco.dance 🐦 @fdans

Francisco Dans is a software engineer living in Madrid whose obsession with the London Underground occasionally drives him to make strange maps.

Dex @ Run For The Hills

runforthehillslondon.com 🐦 @runforthehillls

Dex is a Londoner. An artist and graphic designer, he works in a range of media from hand-crafted illustration to typographic animation.

Dorothy

wearedorothy.com 🐦 @dorothy_uk

Designers of prints, products and other schnizzle.

João Lauro Fonte

laurofonte.com

João Fonte is a Brazilian illustrator and graphic designer living in London.

Julia Forte

Julia Forte has lived in Soho for over 20 years and has a deep interest in London history. Her work includes The Map of London Peculiars *and this map of* London Firsts.

Caroline Harper – Hand-drawn maps

carolineharper.com 🐦 @auntiecazza

Living and working out of her home in south London, Caroline's maps are at once geographical, historical, architectural and mythical. They offer her own view of an area and all that defines it. They help people find their way, and also themselves.

Freya Harrison

freyaillustration.co.uk 🐦 @freyargh

Freya Harrison is a London-based illustrator and designer who likes drawing, maps, pizza and The Smiths.

Ursula Hitz

ursulahitz.com 🐦 @ursulahitz

Ursula Hitz is a London-based graphic designer and artist.

House of Cally

houseofcally.com 🐦 @houseofcally

Cally Lathey is an illustrator and designer. Since graduating from Central Saint Martins, Cally has been producing her own unique style of artwork. Cally's designs are greatly inspired by her childhood growing up in London.

Rebecca Howard Illustration

rebecca-howard.co.uk

Rebecca has illustrated for a number of publishers across the UK, working for companies such as Alistair Sawday and Sustrans. Her artwork has been sold into collections around the world through public exhibitions and galleries in the South of England. She paints and draws from her studio in Berkshire.

Louisa Jones Illustration

louisajonesillustration.com 🐦 @louisajonesillo

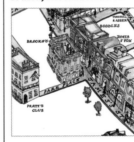

Louisa Jones is a painter, collage artist and printmaker. She studied Illustration at Camberwell College of Arts and since graduating has created bespoke illustrations for Vogue, Paul Smith and Conran, and her work is in the collection of the V&A.

Matt Lancashire

flickr.com/photos/latt/

Matt Lancashire has lived all over London since moving here as a student in 2000. A decade later, inspired by his work at an engineering company, he tried to demonstrate a suspicion that central London has an underlying grid layout.

The London Music Map

londonmusicmap.com 🐦 @LondonMusicMap

The London Music Map was illustrated by RUDE from an original idea by music producer Nick Faber.

Anika Mottershaw

bellaunion.com

Anika Mottershaw is a London-based artist.

Jojo Oldham

lovelyjojos.com 🐦 @lovelyjojos

Jojo Oldham is a jumpsuit-loving creative from the north who lives in southeast London.

Ork Incorporated

orkposters.com

Jenny Beorkrem is a graphic designer and creator of the typographic city neighbourhood map series, working under the moniker Ork Posters since 2007. She lives in Chicago, IL.

Kate Rochester Illustration

katerochester.com 🐦 @KateRoch

Kate Rochester is a designer and illustrator living in Nottingham, whose career has taken in fashion textiles, stationery, and publishing illustration. She specialises in colourful handwriting with excellent hand-drawn, collage, paint and ink skills worked into digital prints.

Jon Rundall & Luke Frost

ifplaceswerefaces.com

Jon Rundall & Luke Frost are part of Heretic, a London-based design and illustration studio specialising in experimental screen printing. They once had a client called Liam from west London, who became Liam Neasden, and the idea grew from there…

Debbie Ryder

debbieryderillustration.com

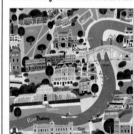

Debbie Ryder is a British artist and illustrator, her graphic, quirky style often inspired by architectural and sporting subjects.

Janina Schröter

janina-schroeter.com

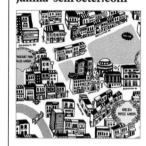

Janina Schröter is a graphic designer and illustrator from Germany who currently works in London. She is specialised in creating hand-drawn maps.

Rewati Shahani

rewatishahani.com 📷 @rewindrave

Rewati Shahani was born and brought up in Mumbai before moving to London, where she has lived for the past 10 years. Her work draws on the relationship between the human and natural worlds, with a particular focus on the cities in which the two collide.

Jane Smith

janeillustration.co.uk/blog 🐦 @DalstonScribble

Jane Smith is a prolific London-based illustrator who draws inspiration from urban life. Architecture and illustrated maps feature frequently in her work although she draws plenty of other subjects too. Jane also enjoys travelling, sketching and printmaking.

Jenni Sparks

jennisparks.com • Print at **evermade.com**

🐦 @jennisparks

Jenni Sparks is an illustrator, designer, map maker, hand-letterer and fun lover. Originally from a small seaside town in southwest England, but now based in east London, she's living the dream of being able to colour stuff in for a living while listening to music all day.

Tilly AKA Running for Crayons

runningforcrayons.co.uk 🐦 @Running4Crayons

Tilly is a smaller-than-average person based in Brighton. She draws inspiration from the everyday and the odd and enjoys creating characters based on the folks around her. Previous clients include The Wall Street Journal, *Visit Britain and Warner Brothers.*

Stephen Walter

stephenwalter.co.uk

Born (1975) in London, Stephen Walter is of English and German heritage. He currently lives and works in London. Walter's art centres on a fascination with the topography of environments and the semiotics of the natural and human cultures that inhabit them. His obsessive drawing techniques often make each work an intricate and layered world in itself. Reproduction courtesy of artist and TAG Fine Arts, London.

Lis Watkins Illustration

lineandwash.co.uk 🐦 @lineandwash

Lis Watkins is a London-based illustrator specialising in watercolour illustration and reportage drawing.

Mark Watkinson

illustrationweb.com

Born in Gloucestershire and growing up in Lincolnshire, Mark originally wanted to be a mechanic. However, one of his teachers suggested he pursue a career in art and he's been a successful freelance illustrator since the early 80s. He plays percussion in a band called the B1200s, collects old cars and enjoys a game of tennis.

Rebecca Lea Williams

rebeccaleawilliams.com 🐦 @RLWArtDesign

Rebecca Lea Williams is an artist and illustrator working in south London. She uses a variety of media; combining watercolour and hand-drawn line work with digital illustration for editorial, branding, publishing and advertising projects, her favourite being maps!

Tom Woolley

tomwoolley.com 🐦 @tcwoolley

Tom Woolley is a freelance illustrator who lives in Bradford, West Yorkshire. Tom specialises in bold and graphic illustrated maps and his clients include Lonely Planet, Computer Arts Magazine, *Europcar and Simon & Schuster publishing.*

CREDITS

Londonist and the Automobile Association would like to thank the following artists and copyright holders for their assistance in the preparation of this book:

4 *Typographic Map of London* © João Lauro Fonte; **7** *Hand Drawn Map of London* © Jenni Sparks. Image courtesy of Jenni Sparks & evermade.com; **9** *The Great London Map* © Rebecca Howard Illustration; **10–11** *A Miscellany of Museums* © Caroline Harper – Hand-drawn maps; **15** *London Parks* © Katherine Baxter. Image courtesy of Katherine Baxter & londontown.com; **17** *Discover the Docklands* © Luke Agbaimoni; **19** *The Waterways and Wildlife of London* © Rebecca Lea Williams; **21** *London Firsts* © Julia Forte; **23** *Maritime Greenwich* © Hartwig Braun; **25** *Brick Lane* © Jane Smith; **26–7** *London Subterranea, 2012* © Stephen Walter. Image courtesy of Stephen Walter & TAG Fine Arts, London; **29** *Mappa Lundi* © Matt Lancashire and reproduced under a Creative Commons license; **31** *Greater London Borough Map* © Ork Incorporated; **32–3** *We Love You London* © Jojo Oldham; **35** *The London Music Map* © The London Music Map; **37** *London Film Map* © Dex @ Run For The Hills; **39** *Illustrated Map of London or Strangers' Guide to the Public Buildings, Theatres, Music Halls and all Places of Interest*, c.1877 (colour litho), Bartlett, G.H. (19th century)(after)/British Library, London, UK/© British Library Board. All Rights Reserved/Bridgeman Images; **41** *Sporting London* © Kate Rochester Illustration; **43** *Book Map* © Dorothy; **45** *Lost London* © Mark Watkinson; **49** *Anglo-Saxon London* © Matt Brown/Londonist; **51** *Ink on paper drawing – House of Flying Rats* © Rewati Shahani; **52–3** *The Thames, London* © Lucie Conoley Illustration; **55** *Gentleman's London* © Louisa Jones Illustration; **57** *South of the River* © Amy Bridges; **58–9** *Bridges of London* © Lis Watkins Illustration; **63** *Plan of the City and Liberties of London after the dreadful conflagration in the year 1666* (engraving), English School, (19th century)/Private Collection/© Look and Learn / Peter Jackson Collection/Bridgeman Images; **65** *River Thames – South West London* © Debbie Ryder; **67** *The Twisted London Underground Map* © Francisco Dans; **69** *The Magnificent Seven* © Freya Harrison; **73** *Sacred River (History of the Thames)* © Katherine Baxter; **75** © *Iguanolondon* Andy Council; **77** *Map of London* © Anika Mottershaw; **79** *London's Secret Gardens* © Janina Schröter; **81** *London's Lost Victorian Buildings* © Bek Cruddace; **82–3** *If Places Were Faces* © Jon Rundall & Luke Frost; **85** *Drink Like a Banker* © Tom Woolley Illustration; **87** *Map of Greater London* © Ursula Hitz; **89** *South East London map* © Tilly aka Running For Crayons; **90–91** *The Illustrated Map of London – second edition* © House of Cally

A note on the maps

Some of the maps displayed here were commissioned by AA Publishing for this book, but the majority of them are the pre-existing work of artists and illustrators drawing the London of their mind's eye. Not all of them are geographically accurate, and not all of them show London as it still exists today; every map is a product of the time at which it was drawn, and of its creator's imagination.

You may notice some differences in spelling between maps, particularly with regard to location of apostrophes: St James's Park and St James' Park, Earls Court or Earl's Court, etc. We have opted not to correct these, and to display the maps as their illustrators originally intended.

A note on the text

All information and esoterica contained within is believed to be correct at the time of printing – or, in the case of more contentious facts, to be supported by at least one additional source. We apologise for any errors you may find and will do our best to correct them in any subsequent editions.

Writing for this title was contributed by

Londonist writers – Tom Bolton, Ellie Broughton, Matt Brown, Joe Carroll, Zoe Craig, Sam Cullen, Daan Deol, Emma Finamore, James Fitzgerald, Rachel Holdsworth, Tabish Khan, Ann Martin, Sian Meades, Will Noble, Joe O'Donnell, Steve Overbury, Beth Parnell-Hopkinson, Laura Reynolds, Matt Roebuck, Harry Rosehill, Hannah Seaton, Rachel Stoplar, Victoria Thomas, Mischa van den Brandhof, Scott Wood and Nick Young.

With special thanks to Daniel Shore, Lydia Manch and Will Noble

Additional writing by Rebecca Needes